To Dorothy,
With best wishes from

Tom Muir

landscapes of
war • peace • nature
scapa flow
tom muir & scapa flow landscape partnership

This book is dedicated to the memory of Dr Anthony Trickett MBE (1940-2013). Tony did an enormous amount for Hoy and Walls in his various roles, from 33 years as island GP to his chairmanship of Longhope Lifeboat Museum Trust and the Hoy Trust. As Lord Lieutenant of Orkney he did much to help commemorate Scapa Flow's history. He will be remembered by many for his enthusiasm and constructive support.

acknowledgements

Thank you to Rita Jamieson and Naismi Flett for sharing their memories of the sinking of HMS *Royal Oak*, and to Mr & Mrs Howard for allowing me to reproduce John J.L. Tulloch's account of the scuttling of the German High Seas Fleet. I am deeply indebted to Bryce Wilson for passing on Frank Davidson's vivid account of an air-raid over Scapa Flow, and my thanks to Mr Davidson and his family for allowing me to use it here. The wonderful photo of the barrage balloon flown from a trawler in Scapa Flow is reproduced courtesy of David Thomas via his webpage, Airgroup4.com, which tells the story of his father's wartime record on the aircraft carrier USS *Ranger*. David was most helpful and sent me a high resolution image to use in this book. Euan Millar kindly let me use the story of the tankard that he had donated to the Scapa Flow Visitor Centre and Museum, which had been a gift to his father. My son, Danny Muir, shared his knowledge of fishing, especially with creels, and the cycle of fisheries throughout the year. David Lynn helped supply information on Fara, both through conversation and on his website. David Mackie and Lucy Gibbon at the Archive Department of the Orkney Library & Archive provided images and access to information crucial in the production of this book. We are very fortunate to have such a valuable resource in Orkney and I cannot thank them enough for the friendly and patient assistance.

Tom Muir, Principal Author

As with every book, there are a great many people to thank and recognise – perhaps more than most given the nature of this book and the area and scheme which it reflects in its pages. The book is the output of one of the 48 projects within the Scapa Flow Landscape Partnership Scheme (SFLPS), which ran from 2009 to 2012. The initial stages of the book project were steered by Anne Bignall, Scapa Flow Ranger / Project Officer for SFLPS. She developed the concept and structure for the book, took on Tom Muir as principal author, and worked particularly with Rebecca Marr and Ken Amer to gather the photographic content around which this book has been based.

Tom Muir, principal author of this book, is a great authority on many aspects of Scapa Flow's heritage, as well as having put a great deal into other SFLPS projects. Geoffrey Stell checked all of the Landscapes of War text whilst Kevin Heath and Andy Hollinrake also assisted in that respect. Brian Budge looked over the page relating to HMS *Royal Oak*, whilst he and Phyllis Gee both commented on the page on HMS *Vanguard*. John Flett Brown kindly reviewed the geology page. I have contributed most of the text for the Projects pages, and I also wrote the 'Echoes of Woodland' page, with help from Jenny Taylor. The sections dealing with Scapa Flow's underwater wildlife were checked by Andrew Want and added to significantly by Anne Bignall.

I have had responsibility for overall editing of the book, and an increasing role in the collation of images and the final compilation, with the help of Anne Bignall and Tom Muir. Final proof reading was undertaken by Clare Gee and Marina Branscombe and it was a pleasure to work with them all, and with Drew Kennedy of The Orcadian who designed the book beautifully.

SFLPS has come about thanks to a range of funders – particularly Heritage Lottery Fund. This book was funded by HLF, Orkney Islands Council and the Scottish Government and European Community Orkney LEADER 2007-2013 programme. In addition, important financial contributions to the Scheme's work were made by the European Regional Development Fund, Historic Scotland, Scottish Natural Heritage, Talisman Energy (UK) Ltd, St Magnus International Festival, RSPB, Robertson Trust, John M Archer Charitable Trust, Hoy Trust and Longhope Lifeboat Museum Trust.

This book relies on its photographs and we are very grateful to those from Ken Amer (Orkney Photographic), Bob Anderson, Raymond Besant, Anne Bignall, Jim Burke, Moira Budge, Roger Davies, Louis Declaro / Orkney Folk Festival, Gerry Cannon, Ian Cunningham, Sheila Faichney, Mark Ferrier, Cathy Fisher, Premysl Fojtu, Sydney Gauld, Joyce Gray, Helen Hadley, Kevin Heath, Andrew Hollinrake, Frances Flett Hollinrake, Imperial War Museum, Rhona Jenkins, Bill Jenman, Colin Keldie, Drew Kennedy, Sarah Lambert, Gareth Lock, Robert MacNamara, Rebecca Marr, Penny Martin, Derek Mayes, Michael Meadows, Eric Meek, Tom Muir, Orkney Media Group, Orkney Research Centre for Archaeology (ORCA), Orkney Skate Trust, Ian Potten, Morris Rendall, Dmitry Rostophin, Kerry Spence, Magnus Spence, Jenny Taylor, David Thomas (Airgroup4.com), Sian Thomas, Sue Whitworth / RSPB, Dan Wise and Chris Wood / Seasearch. The greatest single contribution to the book comes from Orkney Library and Archive, and our thanks go to David Mackie and his colleagues. Our gratitude also goes to Norman Sinclair for the kind use of photos of the Italian POWs taken by his father, James W. Sinclair. The computer-generated image of the wreck of SMS *Brummer* is provided by 3deep Media, who developed www.scapaflowwrecks.com under contract to SFLPS.

Finally, great recognition is due to everyone who helped all the elements of SFLPS come to fruition – the many enthusiastic and inspirational people involved with the projects within the scheme are far too numerous to mention here, but it must always be remembered that they are the very essence of what SFLPS was all about. These individuals and organisations hold the legacy of the scheme, just as they were carrying the torch for Scapa Flow's heritage long before SFLPS was ever thought of.

Without undermining the fundamental role of all those responsible for the work of the individual projects within the Scheme, it is appropriate to take this opportunity to recognise that the Scheme has come about through the leadership and vision shown by the core partnership which took overarching responsibility for the Scheme's funding and governance. The Steering Group consisted of Orkney Islands Council (Gavin Barr, Clare Gee, James Green, Roddy Mackay, Christine Skene & Stuart West all having sat on the group), RSPB (Andy Knight & Eric Meek) and Scottish Natural Heritage (Gail Churchill). The Scheme's implementation team of staff contributed many of the photos. This team comprised Anne Bignall and Joyce Gray throughout, with Sheila Faichney, Cathy Fisher, Bill Jenman and Andrew Purdy being in post for shorter periods.

Julian Branscombe
SFLPS Manager, July 2009 - December 2012

Published by Orkney Islands Council
School Place, Kirkwall, Orkney
KW15 1NY

ISBN 978-1-902957-55-5

© Text: Tom Muir and SFLPS

© Photographs: reproduction rights remain the property of the individual photographers

All rights reserved. The contents of this book may not be reproduced in any form without written permission from the publishers, except for short extracts for quotation or review.

Printed in Orkney by The Orcadian Limited
Hell's Half Acre, Hatston, Kirkwall, Orkney
KW15 1GJ
www.orcadian.co.uk

table of contents

Acknowledgements

Table of Contents
Map
Introduction

Landscapes of War
    1 HMS *Vanguard*
    2 The German Fleet
    3 HMS *Royal Oak*
    4 Air raids
    5 The Churchill Barriers
    6 The Italian Chapel
    7 Coast batteries & boom defences
    8 Lyness
    9 Rinnigill
   10 Golta
   11 Blockships

Landscapes of Peace
   12 Lighthouses
   13 Farming
   14 Fishing today
   15 Fishing history
   16 Barrel of Butter

   17 Oil
   18 Renewable energy
   19 The Orkney Folk Festival
   20 The South Ronaldsay Boys' Ploughing Match
   21 Lifeboats
   22 Ferries
   23 Diving
   24 Island depopulation

Natural Landscapes
   25 Geology
   26 The shaping of a landscape
   27 Echoes of woodland
   28 Whales and dolphins
   29 Seals
   30 Eelgrass
   31 Wreck wildlife
   32 Sandy and muddy bottoms
   33 Seaweed and kelp forests
   34 Flowers
   35 The shore
   36 Birds in summer
   37 Birds in winter

SFLPS Projects

introduction

The name Scapa Flow resonates around the world, thanks to the anchorage's pivotal role in two World Wars. It has held impressive warring fleets since Viking times, and has been a hub for humanity since prehistory. The waters and surrounding land teem with a huge variety of wildlife, including rare and endangered species. The local communities are strong, and Scapa Flow is at the heart of Orkney's vibrant economy. Building styles, boat designs, craft skills and dialect are all aspects of the distinctive cultural heritage.

By 2009, after seven years of development, the Scapa Flow Landscape Partnership Scheme (SFLPS) – led by Orkney Islands Council, Scottish Natural Heritage and RSPB Scotland – had £2m of support pledged for 48 carefully planned projects. Heritage Lottery Fund provided the backbone to this financial package, but 12 other bodies had committed budget to the scheme.

From 2009 to 2012, a team of staff worked with dozens of local heritage organisations and community groups to deliver the 48 funded projects that made up the scheme. Many hours of volunteer creativity, adaptability and commitment went in to each individual project and contributed to the success of the scheme as a whole. This work is carried on into the future by the dedication of these individuals and organisations.

This book tries to capture the essence of Scapa Flow's rich and varied heritage, as well as touching on some of the work undertaken during the three years of SFLPS. The first three sections of the book – Landscapes of War, Landscapes of Peace and Natural Landscapes – reflect the area's broad heritage. It would be a mistake to view each of these in isolation, as it is the interplay between the natural, historic and cultural which makes Scapa Flow's heritage such a pleasure to be involved with.

The final section illustrates some of the SFLPS projects. With 48 well-defined projects, and numerous project strands to some of these – particularly paths, craft projects and interpretation panels – it was never going to be possible to show all of these in the few pages available. However, these project images demonstrate something of the enormous amount that was achieved by so many people, as well as showing further perspectives on the wealth of heritage that is encapsulated by Scapa Flow and surrounds.

Julian Branscombe & Anne Bignall, April 2013

landscapes of war

Balfour Battery, Hoxa Head, South Ronaldsay, with its distinctive twin 6-pounder emplacements and director towers. (Rebecca Marr)

1 HMS Vanguard

On 9 July 1917, HMS Vanguard, a 19,560 ton St Vincent class battleship, blew up at anchor off Flotta in Scapa Flow. She had been on exercise during the day and anchored at her usual position at around 18.30 hours. At 23.20 hours the anchorage was rocked by a huge explosion, followed rapidly by two smaller explosions. HMS Vanguard had not been lost by enemy action but by an internal explosion in one of the ship's magazines, caused either by unstable cordite (the explosive propellant used to fire shells) or by a fire in a neighbouring coal-bunker which caused the cordite to overheat. There were only three survivors of the blast, one of whom later died of his injuries – 843 men lost their lives. The official Inquiry concluded that:

"We consider that the evidence of witnesses of the blowing up of the 'VANGUARD' points to the first visible flame coming up from below just abaft the foremast, this being followed, after a short interval, by a heavy explosion accompanied by a very great increase of flame together with a very large quantity of wreckage fragments thrown up abaft the foremast in the vicinity of 'P' and 'Q' turrets. This explosion was followed after a short interval by a second explosion which considerably increased the volume of flame and smoke (and no doubt debris), but smoke had previously obscured the ship so that the vicinity of this explosion could not be exactly located. The evidence, however, points to it being just abaft the first one."

The hull of HMS Vanguard is launched at Barrow-in-Furness on 22 February 1909. (Private collection)

HMS Vanguard in Scapa Flow. (Orkney Library & Archive)

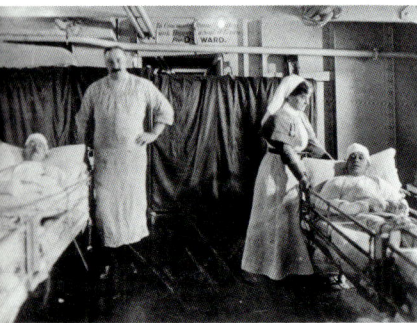

The only two survivors from HMS Vanguard – Private J. Williams RMLI (left) & Stoker 1st Class F.W. Cox (right). (Orkney Library & Archive)

The force of the explosion was so great that wreckage rained down on the neighbouring ships and a naval trawler, which was nearby, was covered in blood and body parts. Private W. Munro, RMLI, on HMS Conqueror told the inquiry that he "...saw the bow and stern of the ship come a little way out of the water while the centre of the ship dropped and then she disappeared, perhaps 7 seconds after the first flame was visible."

Salvage rights were eventually sold to Nundy Marine Metal and work to break up the ship on the seabed began in 1958. Large items were removed, like a twisted propeller shaft and propeller, gun turrets and boilers. Divers wearing hard helmets reported seeing human bones mixed with the coal and oil sludge as they worked among the mangled wreck. Arthur Nundy sold his company in 1971, but salvage work carried on under new owners until the price of scrap metal made it uneconomical. An official war grave buoy was in place by March 1984 but the wreck was not protected by law until 2002.

The HMS Vanguard memorial in the Royal Naval Cemetery at Lyness, "Erected By Relatives and Squadronmates." (Tom Muir)

The buoy marking the wreck site of HMS Vanguard. The wreck is a war grave and diving is prohibited. (Anne Bignall/SFLPS)

2 The German Fleet

The German High Seas Fleet at Wilhelmshaven.
(Orkney Library & Archive)

The 24,700 ton battleship SMS *Kaiser*.
(Orkney Library & Archive)

One of the conditions of the Armistice in 1918 was that Germany surrendered most of its fleet. In late November 1918 the first of the 74 ships of the German High Seas Fleet arrived in Scapa Flow for internment. There they stayed until 21 June 1919 when, under the mistaken belief that the peace talks had broken down, they were scuttled by their own crews. John J.L. Tulloch, born in 1909, was living on Cava at the time and remembered them as a familiar sight.

"…some of them were so near to my home that on a calm day we could hear sailors talking or singing quite clearly. On a Sunday a brass band on the SMS *Friedrich der Grosse* used to play their German military tunes when the weather was good, so those great ships became a part of my childhood days, a source of jetsam that was picked up on my wandering around the shore of my island home."

On the morning of Saturday 21 June 1919 John was on the Calf of Cava when he saw the great ships sink.

"…I saw a flag being hoisted on the flag halyards of the SMS *Friedrich der Grosse*, the ship nearest to the Calf of Cava. When the flag reached its highest point a light breeze caught it for a moment and it fluttered out, the iron cross and double eagle of Germany, then right behind it another red flag climbed the mast but no breeze stirred it, like a piece of old rag it hung in shame. Then across the waters a bell began to ring, clang, clang, clang… it came from one of the ships, either the *Baden* or the *Bayern*. …I gazed around from ship to ship and could see that they were all now either flying flags or in the act of hoisting them, and a great number of the ships were listing over to one side… I was rooted to the spot in fascination as the *Bayern* continued to list further and further until she at last dropped over on her side, hesitated for a few moments before turning upwards, then with a slow motion the bows disappeared under the water, the stern shot up into the air and with a smother of foam and exploding bubbles of air she slid into the depth of Scapa Flow.

…I looked around me and on every side battleships, cruisers and destroyers of the German High Seas Fleet were sinking and boat loads of German sailors were rowing towards Cava. Panic seized me and I commenced to high tail it for home…"

The German High Seas Fleet at anchor around Cava, 28 November 1918.
(Orkney Library & Archive)

A diver starts her exploration of the forward boiler rooms below the decks of the wreck of SMS *Karlsruhe*. (Gareth Lock)

The 28,000 ton battlecruiser SMS *Derfflinger* sinking. (Orkney Library & Archive)

The 25,000 ton battlecruiser SMS *Seydlitz* lying on her side. The salvage company, Cox & Danks, overcame the shortage of coal during the General Strike of 1926 by cutting her open to access her coal bunkers. (Orkney Library & Archive)

The 28,000 ton battlecruiser SMS *Hindenburg* was the only major German ship to sink on an even keel and yet, despite being upright, she proved to be one of the most difficult to salvage. (Orkney Library & Archive)

German Light Cruiser SMS *Nürnberg* ashore on Cava. SMS *Hindenburg* is in the background. (Orkney Library & Archive)

2 The German Fleet

"…The SMS *Seydlitz* was anchored in shallow water therefore did not turn turtle like most of the others, she heaved over on her side and there she lay like a monster whale with one half above water. …The SMS *Moltke* turned turtle near the island of Rysa Little but as she was also in fairly shallow water we could hear the masts and superstructure crunching as it broke with her weight bearing down upon them into the sea bed. When she finally subsided her keel still showed above the water where it could be seen for some time afterwards, but she kept settling down until only her keel showed at low tide. …The SMS *Von der Tann* turned completely turtle and disappeared in a smother of foam…

…The SMS *Derfflinger* was anchored under the cliffs known as The Bring on the island of Hoy, and she made a great fuss about sinking. After listing over and over until she lay on her side then she turned turtle and her stern shot up into the air until she appeared to be standing on her bows, then she dived into the depth below, something aboard her exploded and fountains of water shot into the air, after a little while a second explosion sent more water rocketing out of the sea above her. The water around where she had vanished seethed and boiled for a long time after she had gone. She must have been a mighty Gladiator in battle and such an undignified death was hard to bear.

The SMS *Kaiser* turned over at a great speed. I was watching her turn over and saw a steam pinnace that was in the davits on her off side soar into the air; the fastening ropes broke and it somersaulted over and over slowly in the air before it dropped down into the sea right side uppermost and floated away to drift in below my home and lie on the rocks until my uncle later salvaged it.

…Drifters and destroyers were now busy picking up boat loads of German officers and sailors that were floating around the Flow, cheering as each ship disappeared to her watery grave.

…I was in my glory dragging suitcases, kitbags and boxes out of the sea… My uncle Harry had yoked one of our horses in a cart and he appeared on the scene, we all threw on our findings until the cart was piled high… When we had time to look over our treasures some of them proved to be treasures indeed, there were binoculars, typewriters, bottles of whisky, uniforms with gold braid, flags, chocolate, in fact thousands of things that were priceless. I had found a beautiful officer's dress sword in its scabbard and belt but my uncle spoke me out of it. For weeks afterwards I wore an officer's full dress cap that sat on top of my ears but it had all the gold braid and trimmings that befitted a high ranking officer."

Image of navigable 3D model of the wreck of SMS *Brummer*. www.scapaflowwrecks.com (3deep Media)

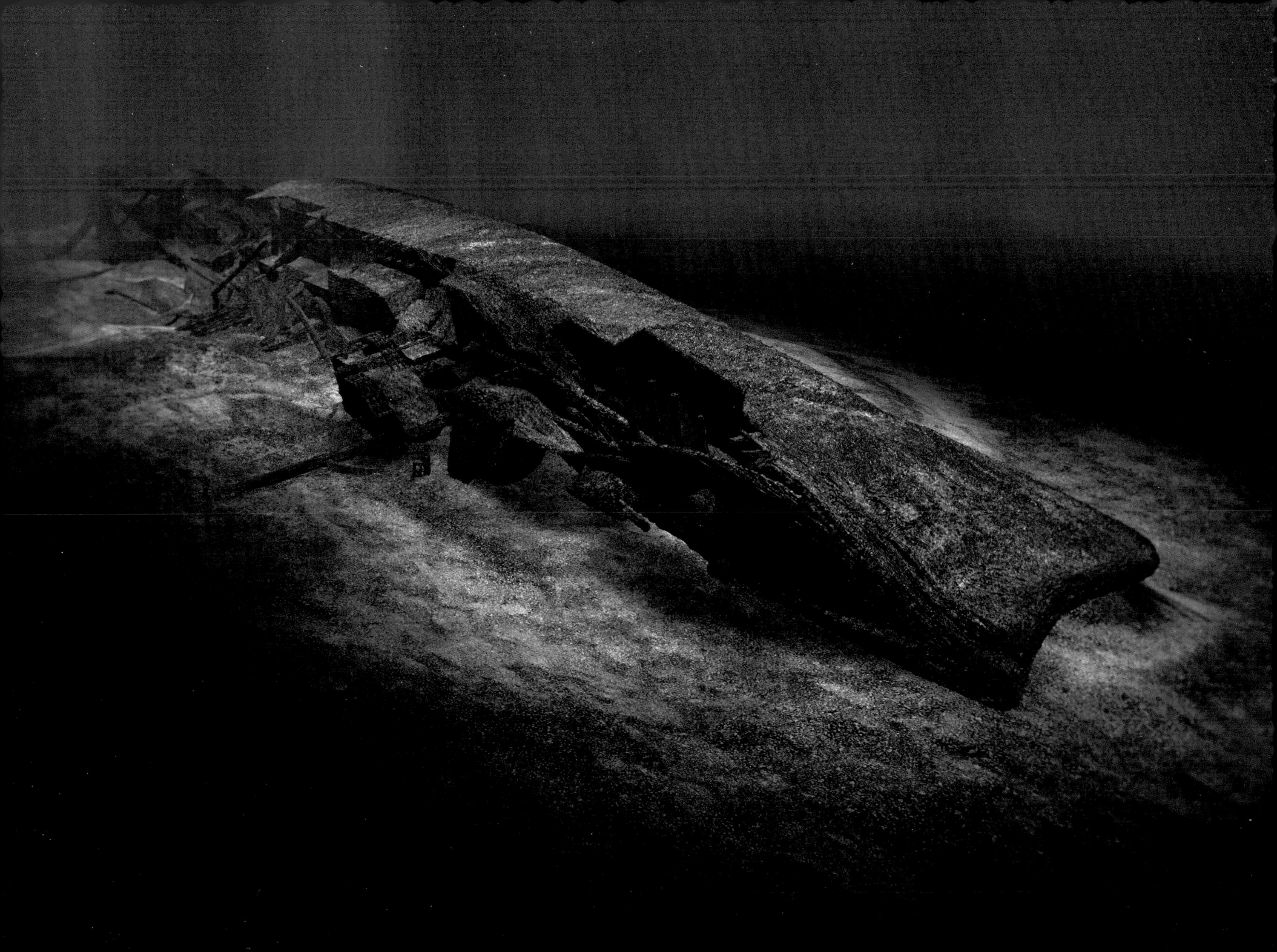

The 25,750 ton battleship HMS *Royal Oak* was a veteran of the Battle of Jutland in World War I. (Orkney Library & Archive)

The view from the bow of HMS *Royal Oak* during a tour of the Mediterranean in the 1920s. (Orkney Library & Archive)

The crew of HMS *Royal Oak* in Malta in the 1920s. Note the bandsmen between the two guns. (Orkney Library & Archive)

Funeral party for victims of HMS *Royal Oak* marching through the Lyness Naval Base on their way to the Royal Naval Cemetery. The survivors of the sinking can be seen wearing boiler suits and plimsolls as they lost their uniforms when the ship sank. (Orkney Library & Archive)

The 517 ton U-boat, *U-47*. (Orkney Library & Archive)

3 HMS *Royal Oak*

At the outbreak of World War II the battleship HMS *Royal Oak* was showing her age. The old veteran of the Battle of Jutland was struggling to keep up with the newer more powerful ships as they patrolled the seas north of Orkney. Suffering some damage after a gale she was sent back to Scapa Flow, almost certainly to provide anti-aircraft cover for the Netherbutton radar station and the eastern side of Scapa Flow. On board were over 160 boy sailors aged between 15 and 17; too young for active service. One of them became friends with Rita Jamieson, whose parents had opened a café near Scapa Pier and whose farm supplied milk to the old battleship. *"We'll sleep well tonight"* he told her, *"we're safe in Scapa Flow."* It was the afternoon of 13 October 1939; the last day of that boy's life.

Kapitänleutnant Günther Prien was sent on a mission to penetrate the defences at Scapa Flow during high tide on the moonless night of 13/14 October 1939. The 31 year old commander eased his submarine, *U-47*, between the blockship *Seriano* and the Holm shore, getting caught in the ship's anchor chain and grounding for a time on the seabed before successfully entering Scapa Flow. He found HMS *Royal Oak* at anchor and attacked, scoring a minor hit to the bow before successfully tearing open the starboard side of the ship with three torpedoes at 01.16 hours. She sank in under 15 minutes – careful cross-checking of military records has now established that 834 lives were lost, around 120 of them being boy sailors. Prien escaped back to Germany and a hero's welcome.

Kapitänleutnant Günther Prien, commander of the *U-47*, receiving the Knights Cross of the Iron Cross from Hitler on his return to Germany. (Orkney Library & Archive)

Naismi Flett lived at Roeberry, three miles from Kirkwall on the Orphir road, at the time of the sinking. She was then four years old and was actually woken by the sound of the torpedo explosions that sank the ship.

"As children we often used to play down on the beach, particularly at Hestigeo, and it was fun among the rocks and the crabs and the pebbles and so on. After the ship sank, it was even more exciting because there were great treasures to be found like brass buttons, sailors' hats, duffel bags, lengths of rope and things like that, which we thought were exciting. We had no sense of any tragedy at all. Nobody said much about the horrific side of it. We were lucky not to find more gruesome things than duffel bags and hats."

Mr Kenneth Toop, the Honorary Secretary of the Royal Oak Association, at a memorial service for his fallen comrades. He was a 16 year-old boy sailor when HMS *Royal Oak* was sunk. (Orkney Photographic)

4 Air raids

A painting of an air raid on Scapa Flow by Sandy Wylie, who was an anti-aircraft gunner. (OIC Collection/Orkney Museum)

Photograph taken from the US Navy aircraft carrier USS *Ranger* of a barrage balloon attached to a trawler in Scapa Flow, 8 September 1943. Note the lightning conductor on the nose of the balloon and the boom defences. (David Thomas/Airgroup4.com)

Ju 88 bomber shot down at Flotterston, Sandwick, on Christmas Day 1940. It flew over Ness Battery during Christmas dinner, but was shot down by a Grumman Martlet from RAF Skeabrae; the first German aircraft to be shot down by an American-built aircraft. All the crew survived and were taken prisoner by Capt. Harcus (carrying an unloaded shotgun), who could speak German as he was a POW in World War I. (Orkney Library & Archive)

On 17 October 1939 the first air attack on the fleet in Scapa Flow saw the old battleship, HMS *Iron Duke*, almost sunk, the first German bomber to be shot down by land-based anti-aircraft guns and the first bomb to land on British soil at Ore Farm, Lyness. On 16 March 1940 James Isbister from the Brig o' Waithe, Stenness, became the first British civilian to die in an air raid. The following month the Scapa Barrage was introduced, when all anti-aircraft guns fired at once for three minutes to blanket the sky with shrapnel. A dramatic description of an air raid in April 1940 was written by the Graemsay crofter, Frank Davidson.

"I became aware of the sound of aircraft. The deep undulating drone was unmistakable. I knew at once that another air-raid was imminent and a glance at the batteries at Scad and Houton confirmed this – their guns were pointing skywards. The anti-aircraft guns from around the base and from the Fleet opened up simultaneously. Throughout the raid they kept an umbrella of flak over the entire Flow. The noise was devastating. The ground trembled and dust fell from roofs and ceilings. Although it was just after sunset the searchlights were also switched on. That, along with the blinding gun-flashes, accentuated the approaching darkness. The scything, swaying beams of the searchlights picked out and attempted to concentrate on what looked like little silver crosses circling and manoeuvring evasively far overhead, perhaps awaiting orders to attack. They dived and came in low, one at a time, at irregular intervals and from different directions. At each attack the machine-guns of friend and foe opened up with their quick-fire rattle. The red tracers crossed again and again as they sped towards the targets with their messages of hate. There was no let up. It went on for about an hour, though it seemed much longer. Scapa Flow was like a huge cauldron, spitting fire and shrapnel, and all around was an inky blackness. Coming in for attack one pilot made a navigational error and was in trouble. In an attempt to clear the surrounding hills the bomb-load was jettisoned, but in moments men and machine were gone. Only ashes and scrap lay scattered on a lonely hill top. The barrage ceased just as suddenly as it had started. The blackness and utter silence was startling. It tended to shock rather than to relieve. Gradually the senses adjusted to reality. The night was not really dark. It was only an hour after sunset. The stars were twinkling in a clear sky and high to the north a gossamer curtain weaved and shimmered – the Aurora Borealis was doing its mystery dance."

James Isbister with his wife Lily on their wedding day. James was the first British civilian casualty of an air raid when the houses at the Brig o' Waithe were bombed on 16 March 1940; he was 27 years old. (Orkney Library & Archive)

A huge crater made by an aerial mine dropped near the YMCA building on Flotta. (Rebecca Marr)

5 The Churchill Barriers

The rock filled wire net 'bolsters' are just breaking the surface of Skerry Sound (No. 2 Barrier), with Lamb Holm in the background, August 1942. (Orkney Library & Archive)

Strong tides rip through Kirk Sound (No. 1 Barrier). (Orkney Library & Archive)

Concrete blocks being cast at the South Burray Blockyard, June 1943. (Orkney Library & Archive)

Winston Churchill was First Lord of the Admiralty at the time of the sinking of HMS *Royal Oak*. He wanted action taken to prevent any more disasters. It was known right from the start where the *U-47* had entered, as the inadequacy of the eastern defences had been highlighted earlier by the Admiral Commanding Orkney and Shetland, Sir Wilfred French, who had offered to take a submarine or a destroyer past the blockships that were supposed to close the channels. His plea for more money was blocked by the Admiralty, who announced that there was to be 'not another penny' spent on blockships for Scapa Flow. Ironically, it was Admiral French who was made the scapegoat for the sinking and placed on the retired list. Following a personal visit in March 1940, Churchill ordered that the four channels to the east of Scapa Flow had to be closed permanently. More blockships were also sunk as a temporary measure.

A million tons of rock and concrete would go into the construction of the Barriers that bear the name of the man who ordered their construction. On 10 May 1940, the 16,000 ton liner *Almanzora* arrived to act as temporary accommodation for workers and her holds were full of work materials. It was a huge undertaking; piers had to be built, work camps erected and quarries opened.

Overhead cableways (called 'Blondins' after the famous 19th century tightrope walker 'The Great Blondin') were set up on either side of the channels to carry the rock-filled bags, called 'bolsters' that were dropped along the length of the channel to form the core of the Barrier. After the rocky core was in place concrete blocks were placed over it in a 'pell-mell' formation to disperse the force of the waves. This design was chosen as a result of experiments carried out in test tanks at Manchester University.

Workers came from all over the UK and even the Republic of Ireland. Many men found the weather and the feeling of isolation in an alien landscape too much to endure and demanded to be sent home; an option not open to the sailors on the ships nearby in Scapa Flow. Many Irish workers were also returned home after pro-IRA graffiti was found in one of the accommodation huts. In 1942 Italian POWs were brought in as labourers, but went on strike as they considered that the work was of a warlike nature, in breach of the Geneva Convention. A meeting between prisoners and local officials agreed that these were not defences but actually causeways for civilian use, and so work continued. The Barriers were so secret that people in the North Isles of Orkney didn't hear about them until the war was over.

The rubble core of No. 3 Barrier closes East Weddell Sound, August 1942. (Orkney Library & Archive) ▶

Maintenance work on No. 2 Barrier. The engine of the blockship *Lycia* can be seen in the sea on the right. (Joyce Gray/SFLPS) ▶

6 The Italian Chapel

The chapel as it was when it was first built. (James W. Sinclair)

Italian POWs gather around Chiocchetti's statue of St George and the Dragon. (James W. Sinclair)

Chiocchetti at work restoring the chapel during a return visit in 1960. (James W. Sinclair)

Italian POWs outside the chapel. Chiocchetti is standing on the far left and Palumbi stands in front of the left pillar. (James W. Sinclair)

In February 1942 over 1000 Italian POWs arrived in Orkney to work on the building of the Barriers. They were held in two camps, Camp 34 in Burray and Camp 60 in Lamb Holm. The bleak, uninhabited island of Lamb Holm was a far cry from the deserts of North Africa where the Italians had been captured. The artist Domenico Chiocchetti recalled the scene.

> "The little island could hardly have appeared more desolate: bare, foggy, exposed to the wind and heavy rain. The camp consisted of thirteen dark, empty huts and mud."

Chiocchetti had put his artistic training to good use by creating a sculpture of St George slaying the dragon, made out of concrete over a barbed wire frame, as a centrepiece that stood in the camp square. When Italy capitulated to the Allies in 1943 the POWs were still not free to go home, but they were now paid for the work that they did and had a certain amount of freedom of movement.

The arrival of a priest in the camp was the catalyst for Chiocchetti to reveal his dream of building a chapel. He had been trained as a painter of churches and now he wanted to create a church of his own, not just for himself but for all the prisoners. Two Nissen huts were put at his disposal and he had them joined together to form a long building. A team of volunteer workers was recruited, including the blacksmith Giuseppe Palumbi, who made the beautiful rood screen designed by Chiocchetti. The outside was covered with wire 'bolster' nets and concrete and scrap was used to create the fittings. Lanterns were made from cut up bully-beef tins, candlesticks from stair carpet holders, floor tiles courtesy of the toilet of the blockship *Ilsenstein* and the wood for the tabernacle was also taken from a blockship.

Chiocchetti's masterpiece is undoubtedly the altarpiece painting of the Madonna and Child. The whole symbolism of the chapel is about peace and understanding among people. Although the POWs didn't stay for long enough to really use the chapel, it was actually the building of it that was the important part. It remains as a symbol of peace from a dark time in world history and is an inspiration to all who visit it, regardless of their religion or lack of it.

Chiocchetti shows his artistic masterpiece to his wife, Maria, during a visit in 1964. (James W. Sinclair)

Interior of the Italian Chapel on Lamb Holm. (Drew Kennedy)

American-made coast defence gun guarding Hoy Sound on the site of the present Stromness Golf Course in World War I. (Orkney Library & Archive)

World War I searchlight battery on Flotta. (Orkney Library & Archive)

Six-inch gun at Stanger Head, Flotta, after World War II. (Orkney Library & Archive)

Six-inch gun at Ness Battery after World War II. (Orkney Library & Archive)

7 Coast Batteries & Boom Defences

Substantial defences were required for Scapa Flow after it was chosen as the Royal Navy's main anchorage at the start of each World War – 1914 and 1939 both marked the start of extended periods of frenetic activity to put proper protection in place for the Fleet.

The main entrance into Scapa Flow was through Hoxa Sound. This was defended in both World Wars by coast batteries at Hoxa Head in South Ronaldsay and Stanger Head in Flotta. These batteries had 6-inch guns that could engage enemy ships at a range of up to seven miles.

Any attacking ships getting past these big guns came up against boom defence nets. Further gun batteries were positioned to pound ships that were stopped or slowed by the boom. In World War I, the Hoxa Sound boom was defended by four 4-inch quick-fire guns positioned at Hoxa and another four across the Sound at Stanger Head. In World War II, fearsome twin 6-pounder guns – two pairs at Balfour Battery near Hoxa Head and a single pair at Buchanan Battery on Flotta – defended the boom. If enemy motor-torpedo-boats tried to storm the boom, using their speed to attempt to skip over them, they would be in the arcs of fire of these guns for three minutes, in which time over 400 high explosive rounds could be fired into them.

The main booms comprised a steel wire-mesh curtain to block submarine access, supported by a stout hawser held afloat by rows of large rectangular wooden floats and boom boats. Each float contained a pair of galvanised air-filled steel tanks. After the war these floats were broken up and a hole cut in the top of the tanks which were then sold to farmers as water troughs for cattle. The remains of four of the wooden floats (minus their tanks) are still to be seen at the Burray end of No. 3 Barrier.

Behind the main boom defence nets there was a second anti-submarine net. The anti-submarine boom used during World War I stretched from Roan Head in Flotta to Nevi Skerry and then on to Hunda. This was protected by four 12-pounder guns in a battery at Roan Head at the tip of Golta, Flotta. During World War II the boom stretched from the Calf of Flotta to Hunda; the remains of these nets can still be seen lying in the sea between Flotta and the Calf of Flotta.

In both World Wars, the boom defences were backed up by indicator loops on the seabed that could detect a large metal object passing overhead and by hydrophones to listen for the sound of engines. If an enemy U-boat was detected a minefield could be remotely detonated. This was the fate of the *UB-116*, which tried to breach the defences on 28 October 1918 in a last, desperate

◀ WRNS making anti-submarine boom defence nets, Lyness, World War II. (Orkney Library & Archive)

View across Hoy Sound to Stromness & Graemsay from the Battery Observation Post of Skerry Battery, Hoy. (Rebecca Marr) ▶

Anti-submarine hurdles built across Clestrain Sound in World War I.
(Orkney Library & Archive)

World War I Boom Defence Depot in St Margaret's Hope, South Ronaldsay.
(Orkney Library & Archive)

Boom defence laying vessel.
(Orkney Library & Archive)

Boom defences at Hoxa Sound, World War II.
(Orkney Library & Archive)

7 Coast Batteries & Boom Defences

attempt to sink British warships. It was commanded by Kapitänleutnant Hans Joachim Emsmann. He was assured that there was no minefield but in reality it was to prove a suicide mission. The destruction of *UB-116* was reported in The Orcadian on 12 December 1918:

> "The enemy craft was detected near the entrance, however – possibly her presence was first divulged with the aid of the wonderful hydrophone – and when the vessel came over a minefield controlled electronically from a shore station mines were exploded. Other measures were immediately taken to make doubly sure of the entire destruction of the U-boat. A number of bodies were subsequently recovered, and a portion of the conning tower, which was salved and taken to St. Margaret's Hope, was an object of intense interest to the islanders."

The other entrances to Scapa Flow were also defended by indicator loops, controlled minefields, boom nets and coast batteries. World War I also saw the construction of a series of steel 'hurdles' across the western approach to Scapa Flow, in addition to the boom defence net from Houton Head in Orphir to Scad Head in Hoy.

During World War II, an impressive series of coast batteries was developed along Hoy Sound. The first to be put in place was Ness Battery with its two 6-inch guns. This battery, including its unique accommodation huts, has been conserved and is open for tours, giving the public the chance to experience what is now Britain's most important coast battery.

Ness Battery became the Fire Command for the six batteries running from the mouth of Hoy Sound to the boom between Houton Head and Scad Head. The twin 6-pounder battery at Scad Head was notable for being supplied by wagons winched down rails set on the steep slope from the road above.

The concentration of defences that were put in place in World War I and II, and the extent to which they have survived, make Scapa Flow unparalleled around the world for the quantity and quality of its wartime archaeology.

◀ A mess hut decorated for Christmas, World War II.
(Orkney Library & Archive)

Anti-submarine boom defence nets between Flotta and the Calf of Flotta. In the foreground is a boom-laying pontoon. (Rebecca Marr) ▶

HMS *Pomona* Boom Defence Depot at Lyness. (Orkney Library & Archive)

Boom defence nets being towed from Lyness; note the oil tanks in the background. (Orkney Library & Archive)

WRNS signal messages to the ships in Scapa Flow from the roof of the Wee Fea Communications Centre. (Orkney Library & Archive)

Tugs and small vessels alongside the West Pier, Lyness. (Orkney Library & Archive)

8 Lyness

Lyness was first used by the Royal Navy as an oil depot in 1917 when four oil tanks with the capacity to hold 12,000 tons of fuel oil were built in response to ships converting from the use of coal to oil. In 1919 it became the Naval HQ in Orkney and in line with naval procedure it was given a ship's name, HMS *Proserpine* (known unflatteringly as 'Properswine' by those serving there). By the late 1930s work began to enlarge the base, with a further twelve above ground oil tanks built. Oil was shipped in by tanker and pumped into these tanks with steam powered pumps situated in the Pumphouse which is now the Scapa Flow Visitor Centre & Museum. Later six massive tanks with the capacity to hold 100,000 tons of oil were built underground, inside Wee Fea Hill above Lyness. Oil in the 16 above ground tanks was warmed up with heating elements, rather like the one in an electric kettle, until it became more fluid and then was pumped up the hill by a diesel pumping station situated half way up. Oil could then be pumped back down the hill as needed.

Earth and rock debris from the construction of the underground tanks was used in the construction of a wharf, which was locally called the 'Golden Wharf' due to its £35,000 price-tag. Piers and slipways were built in Ore Bay to serve the naval ferry, drifters and tug boats. Boom Defence Command, called HMS *Pomona*, also had its base here; a huge concreted area in front of the Pumphouse being used to repair damaged anti-submarine nets. Just offshore was moored the former liner, *Dunluce Castle*, which acted as the Drifter Pool HQ under the name HMS *Pleiades*.

Lyness was like a boom town in 1940, with over 12,000 military and civilian personnel living in camps. A new Naval Communications Centre was built on Wee Fea Hill, coming into service in September 1943. By January 1945 it was handling around 25,000 messages a day, from telephone calls, visual signals by Morse lamp and by teleprinter. There was even a telephone link to the buoy where the flagship was moored so that the Admiral could speak directly from his ship to the War Office in London. Of the 270 staff that ran the Communications Centre, 230 were women. By 1943 there were some 1500 WRNS stationed at Lyness. It was noted that the appearance of the camps, and indeed the servicemen, improved greatly as a result of the influx of women!

The North Pier at Lyness, completed in January 1941, was used by the naval ferries that linked the South Isles with the Mainland, also for landing stores and by sailors departing or returning from leave. (Tom Muir)

Aerial view of the Crockness Martello Tower showing the square base of the World War II radar installation. (Orkney Library & Archive)

The remains of the egg-like structure of the Torpedo Attack Trainer. (Rebecca Marr)

Rinnigill Fire Fighting Station. (Orkney Library & Archive)

Rinnigill Radar Centre. (Orkney Library & Archive)

Aerial view showing the Lyness oil tanks in the 1970s. In the foreground is the pier at Rinnigill with the salvage crane alongside. (Orkney Library & Archive)

9 Rinnigill

Rinnigill lies on the opposite side of Ore Bay from Lyness. Here are a collection of strange looking buildings in various states of decay that were once research, training, supply and maintenance installations. It began with a hydrogen production plant for the RAF Balloon Command to create the gas needed to keep more than 80 barrage balloons up in the air. A pier was built in 1941 where supplies and hydrogen bottles were landed. A Fire Fighting School was then built, opening on 6 July 1942 and taking 30 classes a day. Training covered how to tackle any type of fire onboard a ship and was held in a number of concrete huts designed to resemble the inside of a ship.

At the time of writing, the remains of floating crane GWR 30, which belonged to Dougall Campbell and David Nicol, the men who had bought Nundy Marine Metals in 1971, lie on the shore in front of these buildings. Their purchase included 20 acres of land in Flotta, along with the old cinema, and 25 acres of land at Rinnigill with sheds and the former RAF pier, where salvaged scrap metal was landed. The coal-fired, stiff-leg steam crane could lift 50 tons, but couldn't move independently and had to be towed to the salvage site.

A top secret radar centre was established at Rinnigill in 1943, replacing a smaller operation that had taken place at Lyness. Here ships' radar sets were repaired and people were trained to operate them in the five classrooms and lecture cinema brought into service by early 1945. A naval radar scanner was erected on top of the nearby Crockness Martello Tower (which dates from the Napoleonic Wars). The dishes from the radar were later used by farmers as drinking troughs for cattle. Radar maintenance work reached a peak in 1944 in the run up to D-Day, as all ships were fitted with new improved radar sets called CXFR. It was crucial for the invasion that these sets were working perfectly and that the operators knew how to use them.

Above the complex is a Torpedo Attack Trainer for pilots. Inside was a timber structure covered with plaster, 14m in diameter by 7.5m high, which gave one the impression of being inside a gigantic egg. The pilot sat in a mock aeroplane cockpit in the centre while a horizon with a ship's silhouette was projected onto the walls that surrounded him. Here pilots from RNAS Twatt (HMS *Tern*) could practice torpedo-bomber attacks. The roof has now gone and the plaster walls have crumbled. The egg-like interior later saw use as a 'wall of death' by local boys on motorbikes, until one of them went through the door!

World War II buildings at Rinnigill. (Rebecca Marr)

Interior of the World War I YMCA building. (Orkney Library & Archive)

Loading a rocket at the Flotta Z Battery. (©Imperial War Museum H-039436)

Boxing Tankard won by 'Smudger' Smith in Flotta; now on display at the Scapa Flow Visitor Centre & Museum, Lyness. (Orkney Museum)

10 Golta

The peninsula of Golta in Flotta contains a rare example of a World War II anti-aircraft Z Battery. Here 64 rocket launchers, supplied by 128 magazines, could fire a barrage of rockets some 22,000 feet (6700m) into the air, bursting to shower the sky with deadly shrapnel. The crumbling magazines, looking like miniature Nissen huts, are corrugated iron shelters covered in concrete with concrete filled sandbags used to build the front. In these shelters were mobile racks containing 3-inch diameter rockets.

The remains of the old YMCA building dominate Golta. Built in 1917 it cost a colossal £6,954 19s, but it provided much needed recreational facilities to go along with the nearby golf course which was used by Admiral Jellicoe and King George V. It was outside the YMCA that the annual Grand Fleet Boxing Championship was held in World War I.

Wartime had the strange effect of both reinforcing and breaking down class barriers, as shown by the story of a World War II pewter tankard that was donated to the Scapa Flow Visitor Centre and Museum by Euan Millar.

"My father, Robert Millar, was a teacher of English in Hamilton, Scotland, before World War II. Shortly before war broke out he joined the Officer Training Corps and then progressed through the ranks until around 1942/43 he spent a year as Adjutant with the Royal Artillery anti-aircraft unit stationed at Lyness. In such an exalted position he had his own batman (man servant), one 'Smudger' Smith from Birmingham. Like many ordinary soldiers at the time Smudger was semi-literate, however, he was very handy with his fists! He had quite a number of tankards to show for it. The nights were quite busy with guns blasting away but the days could be long, so my father, to keep his hand in at teaching, started to teach his loyal batman to read and write. When the time came for my father to be posted away from Scapa Flow, Smudger, who did not have much, gifted this tankard to my father as a thank you. It has remained in my family ever since. They kept in Christmas card touch after the war, but met again only once, when in the early 1960s a family motoring holiday to Devon was diverted through the back streets of Birmingham so they could meet. My brother and I have a vivid memory of my father, a tall, refined, formal Head of the English Department at an Edinburgh ladies' college, and a short working class man from Birmingham leaping around like schoolboys at the sight of one another after 20 years!"

Rockets being fired from the Z Battery, Flotta (©Imperial War Museum H-039435)

The ruins of the World War I YMCA building on Golta, Flotta. (Rebecca Marr)

World War I blockships in Burra Sound with the Black Craig of Stromness in the background.
(Orkney Library & Archive)

World War II blockships in Kirk Sound, taken from Lamb Holm with St Mary's Village, Holm, in the background.
(Orkney Library & Archive)

World War II blockships *Lycia* and *Ilsenstein* in Skerry Sound, taken from No. 2 Barrier. These ships were sources of material used in the construction of the Italian Chapel; floor tiles from the *Ilsenstein's* toilet were used in front of the altar.
(Orkney Library & Archive)

Salvage work being carried out on the blockships in Water Sound after the war. In the centre we see the *Carolina Thorden* (sister ship of the *Johanna Thorden*, which was wrecked on the Pentland Skerries and Swona in 1937) being pumped out. The oil tanker *Juniata* is beached on the sand at South Cara, South Ronaldsay; she was later cut in two and her bow section towed to Inganess Bay where it remains, just below the airport.
(Orkney Library & Archive) ▶

11 Blockships

Blockships were sunk in both World Wars, at Kirk, Skerry, East Weddell and Water Sounds in the east and Burra Sound in the west. They were a rich source of plunder to local people. One of the World War I blockships in Burra Sound contained a piano, which ended up in a cottage in Graemsay. The *Reginald*, which still lies in East Weddell Sound, was completely stripped of non-ferrous metal as she rolled over from side to side with the ebb and flow of the tide until her hull finally broke in two.

After World War I there were appeals to the Admiralty to remove the blockships as access to fishing grounds had been cut off by them. In March 1920 tragedy struck when two Burray men and a girl from Hunda were drowned in Skerry Sound when their boat was caught in the strong currents that swirled around the blockships. Two survivors managed to climb onto a blockship but their desperate waving was at first ignored by people in St Mary's village as they thought they were inspectors from the Admiralty that had been looking at the wrecks. Following this accident, one Kirk Sound blockship, *Numidian*, was swung around out of the channel and the *Aorangi* was raised and taken away, only to break its tow line and become wrecked on the Holm shore. In Water Sound the *Lorne* was finally blown up in 1931.

In World War II many more blockships were sunk. The *Carron* was run aground on Burray by the ship's crew, who enjoyed their breakfast before leaving, dirty dishes still on the table. Once again the blockships became a highly valued resource. In 1939 a group of wreckers found themselves in court after stripping metal from the *Seriano*, which included part of a compressor used by Metal Industries Ltd to operate her anchor chain. The *Ilsenstein* in Skerry Sound was found to have a hole in her side large enough for a yole to get through. One wrecker found to his dismay that the tide had come in while he was stripping metal and the hole was now under water so he had to wait for the tide to ebb before getting out.

The *Inverlane* lost her stern to a mine in 1939 and lay at Longhope until she was sunk in Burra Sound in 1944. She was used for fire fighting practice, but a man was killed during one practice and his body was never found. Local men found the body when they were stripping metal from the ship, but if they had reported it to the authorities they would've been in trouble. Their predicament was solved when the ship was towed away to be sunk soon after. Many blockships were broken up for scrap in the late 1940s.

The World War I blockship *Reginald*, which once sailed between Liverpool and Dublin, lies on its side in East Weddell Sound. In the foreground are the wooden casings for large boom defence floats.
(Drew Kennedy) ▶

landscapes of peace

Hoy Low Lighthouse, Graemsay.
(Orkney Library & Archive)

Hoy Low Lighthouse, Graemsay.
(Orkney Library & Archive)

Hoy High Lighthouse, Graemsay.
(Orkney Library & Archive)

12 Lighthouses

The Hoy Sound, which leads to Stromness and Scapa Flow, has always been a treacherous piece of water. On the south side is the Bow Rock of Hoy while to the north lie the Kirk Rocks; dangerous reefs submerged at high tide. Appeals to the Northern Lighthouse Board for some form of assistance in navigating these hazards resulted in the building of two lighthouses on the island of Graemsay, Hoy Sound High and Hoy Sound Low.

These lighthouses were designed by the engineer Alan Stevenson (1807-1865) and built by Alexander Wilson, who employed Irish workmen in their construction. Accommodation 'bothies' had to be built, along with a slipway at the Bay of Sandside where the building blocks were landed. Originally the stone was quarried in Hoy, but it was found to be too soft for the task and so rock was brought in from the North Isles instead. The stone was shaped and prefabricated on a circular base at Point of Ness by Stromness, and the interlocking stones transported to Graemsay for erection. Hoy High (as it is popularly called) is a beautiful, elegant structure on the east side of the island, 115 feet (35m) tall. Hoy Low on the west coast is 56 feet (17m) in height. The lighthouse keepers' houses at both lighthouses are unusual in their design which is based on that of an Egyptian temple.

These lighthouses are 'leading lights' to guide ships through the safe deepwater channel. The low light is seen as a fixed white light while the high light is a fixed red one. By lining up the one light above the other you know that you are in the safe channel. Once the high light is obscured by the land it is time to turn northwards towards Stromness.

Hoy High Lighthouse, Graemsay.
(Orkney Library & Archive)

The old Hoxa Beacon, South Ronaldsay. (Orkney Library & Archive)

The Hoy High lighthouse is also seen as a flashing red or white light, depending on your position. They were first lit on the evening of Thursday 15 May, 1851. They were automated in 1966.

At the other end of Scapa Flow is the Cantick Head lighthouse in South Walls, built in 1858 and designed by Alan Stevenson's brothers, David and Thomas (the father of the writer Robert Louis Stevenson). It was automated in 1991; its lens (which was strafed by a Luftwaffe aircraft during World War II) can be seen on display at the Scapa Flow Visitor Centre and Museum.

Minor lights on other islands and navigational lights on buoys supplement the principal lights on Graemsay and at Cantick Head.

Hoy High Lighthouse, Graemsay. (Tom Muir)

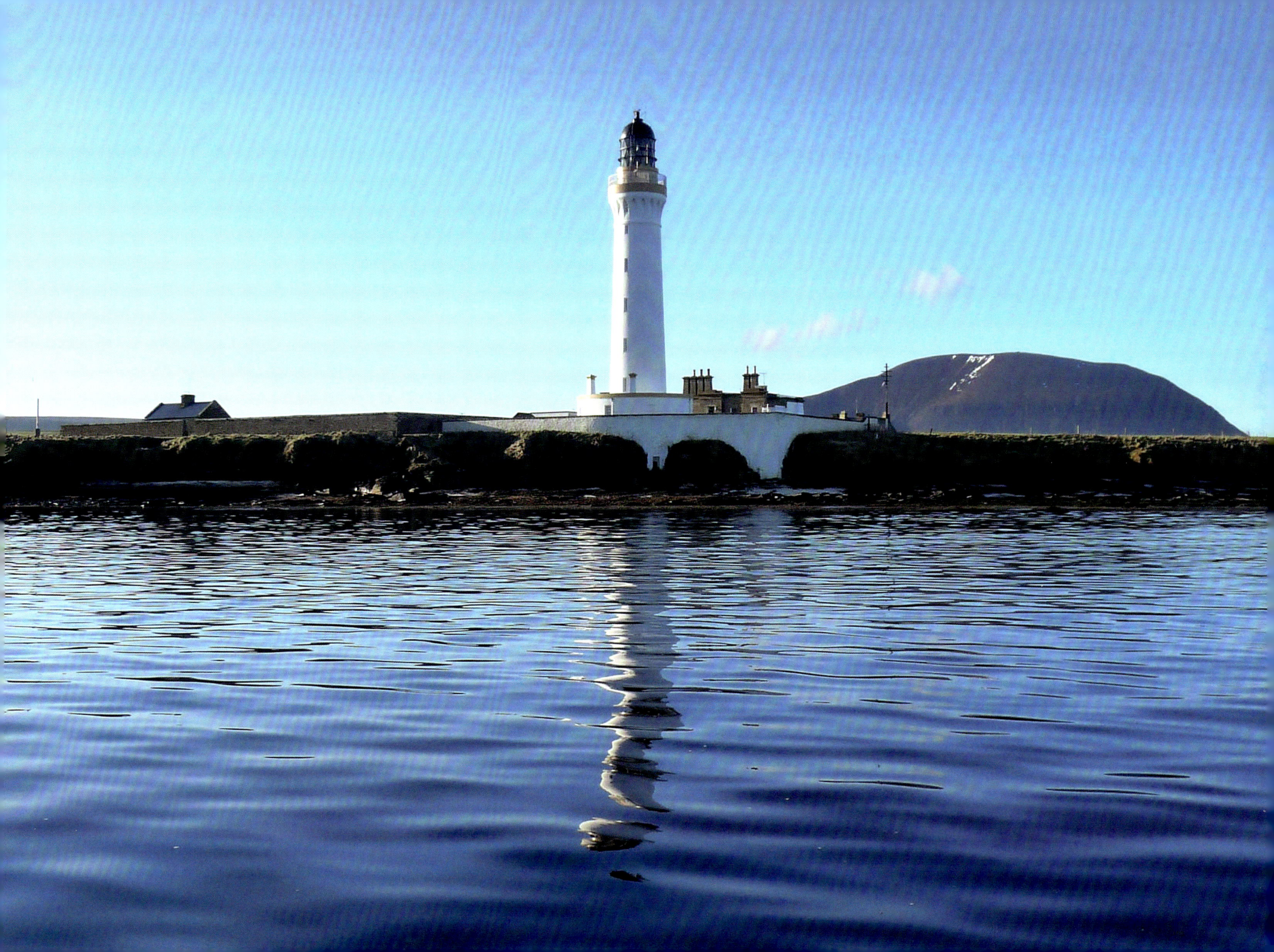

Ploughing with an ox, Hoy. (Orkney Library & Archive)

Ox drawn reaper cutting oats in Hoy, looking across to Graemsay with Black Craig behind in the far distance. (Orkney Library & Archive)

Carting in sheaves of oats to build into stacks, Garson, Stromness (Orkney Library & Archive)

13 Farming

Farming is hugely important to the Orcadian economy these days, with Orkney beef and lamb being prized for its high quality. Farmers cut silage and grow barley for winter fodder. But the green landscape that we see today was not always like that. If we had sailed into Scapa Flow 200 years ago we would have seen more brown than green as the moorland and hills were uncultivated and undrained. Heather grew in abundance on the hills as well as on the land around Hobbister in Orphir. The deep deposits of peat – the remains of plants, particularly *Sphagnum* moss, preserved in acid waterlogged conditions – were cut, dried and used for fuel.

A good example of what happened in the mid 19th century is the Swanbister estate in Orphir. Subsistence crofters, renting from the laird, cultivated bere, a primitive form of barley in a run-rig system. Each family had strips of land of varying quality scattered over a wide area. Their houses were built in 'toonships' next to the arable land, surrounded by the turf walls of the 'hill dykes', outside of which cattle and sheep grazed on the commonly held hills.

When Swanbister was bought by the Devonshire man, Archer Fortescue, in 1845 he set about modernising the land, much to the annoyance of his crofters and neighbouring farmers. He built himself and his new wife a grand house and started squaring the land into farms, breaking up the old toonship. He built houses for his servants who lived there rent free, but their new homes depended on their work for the laird. He ploughed out moors and received a Government grant of £1,000 to drain land, reclaiming 80 acres of saltmarsh which was sectioned off into fields and enclosed with stone dykes. He also used flagstones set on edge as walling to shelter cattle, while he also claimed the common ground of the hill for a flock of Cheviot sheep. If any animals strayed onto his hill land he would impound them and only return them after a fine was paid, earning him the nickname *'the Devil of the Hills'*.

To improve the land he used rotted down seaweed, Peruvian guano, bone meal, lime and 3,000 tons of 'town dung' which was boated in from Stromness in the first ten years of improvements. He also built the pier at Swanbister Bay for steamships to call from Aberdeen and take away cattle that had been sold to dealers. The pier was extended in World War I with a crane added on the end for transporting aircraft from the nearby air station to ships in Scapa Flow. Fortescue's methods were not universally popular, but agricultural improvement was the path that Orkney would follow into the modern age.

Horse drawn binder cuts oats and binds it into sheaves. (Orkney Library & Archive)

Fields of oat stooks ready to be carted home, Orphir. (Orkney Library & Archive)

Cattle on Burray; the remains of the blockships *Empire Seaman* and *Martis* can be seen in the extreme right of the image, just in front of Glimps Holm. (Rebecca Marr)

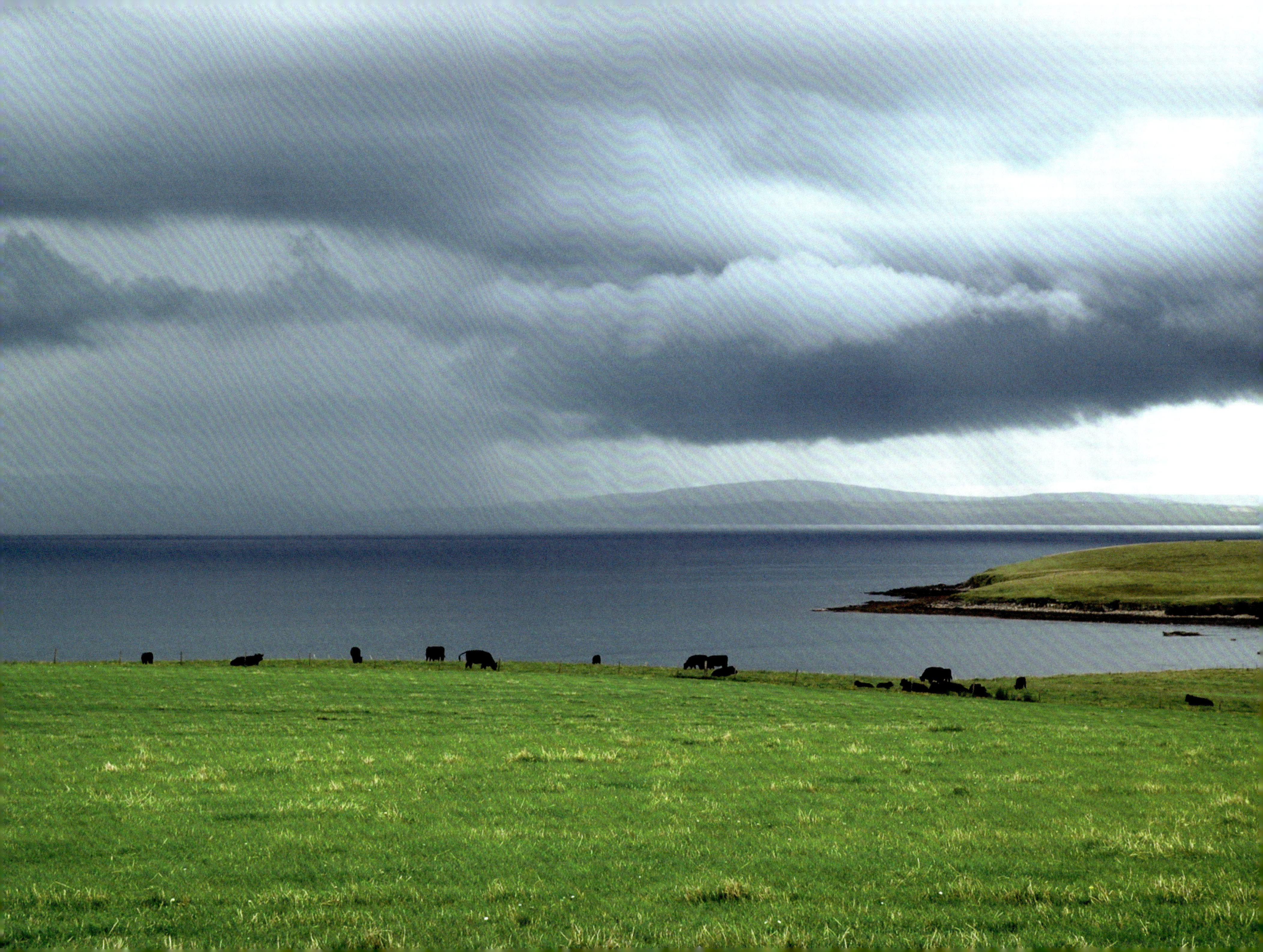

St Margaret's Hope – no longer a busy fishing village but now home port for Pentland Ferries' mv *Pentalina*. (Raymond Besant)

Creels with Stromness beyond. (Rebecca Marr)

Creel fishing off Hoxa Head. (Rebecca Marr)

14 Fishing today

The most active fishery in Scapa Flow is for crabs and lobsters, which are caught in creels – wire and nylon string cages that trap the unwary crustacean. Creels are set around the islands in areas favoured by lobsters and brown crabs (called 'partans' in Orkney). Partans have only come into their own during the 20th century. Before that, local fishermen were setting creels for lobsters and the partans were looked on as little more than a pest; many were killed and thrown overboard while some were taken home for the pot, but never sold. Now they are a delicacy and are exported worldwide, especially to Spain. Since the 1980s velvet crabs have also been sold and now green crabs as well.

Partans are more common during the summer months while lobsters are mostly caught in the late summer and early autumn. Most lobsters will migrate to deeper water during the winter while partans remain in their usual habitat but are less active. The law in Scotland states that a 'berried' lobster (a female carrying eggs) can be landed. However many creel fishermen conduct a voluntary 'notching' system where a 1cm V-shaped notch is cut into the tail. This will grow out naturally after about three years, but fishermen are not allowed to sell lobsters marked like this, which protects the breeding females and sustains lobster numbers.

Prawns live in the muddy-bottomed areas of Scapa Flow and are caught at night by a net dragged along the seabed. Trawling for great and queen scallops forces the scallops to rise through the sediment to be caught in a net, however this causes great disruption to the seabed habitat. Now many scallops are hand-caught by divers, which is more sustainable, and gives a product that rightfully commands a premium price.

Fish farms raising salmon are now becoming more common and bring money and jobs to Orkney, but they are controversial. There have been protests from sea trout anglers who blame fish farms for infestations of sea lice – parasites that eat into the skin and flesh of fish – in the wild sea trout. One of the main problems that face fish farms is seals, which can attack nets and kill fish. Effective anti-predator nets are expensive, whilst some anti-predator nets have entangled and killed seals and diving birds. With licences needed to shoot seals, some fish farms have had to kill salmon early to cut their losses. It is a highly emotive issue.

Fish farm – illuminated at night to promote the development of healthy fish – off the Orphir coast; two oil tankers and the Holm coast beyond. (Derek Mayes)

◀ Fish farm off Rysa Little. (Rebecca Marr)

Creel on the pier at St Mary's, Holm. (Raymond Besant) ▶

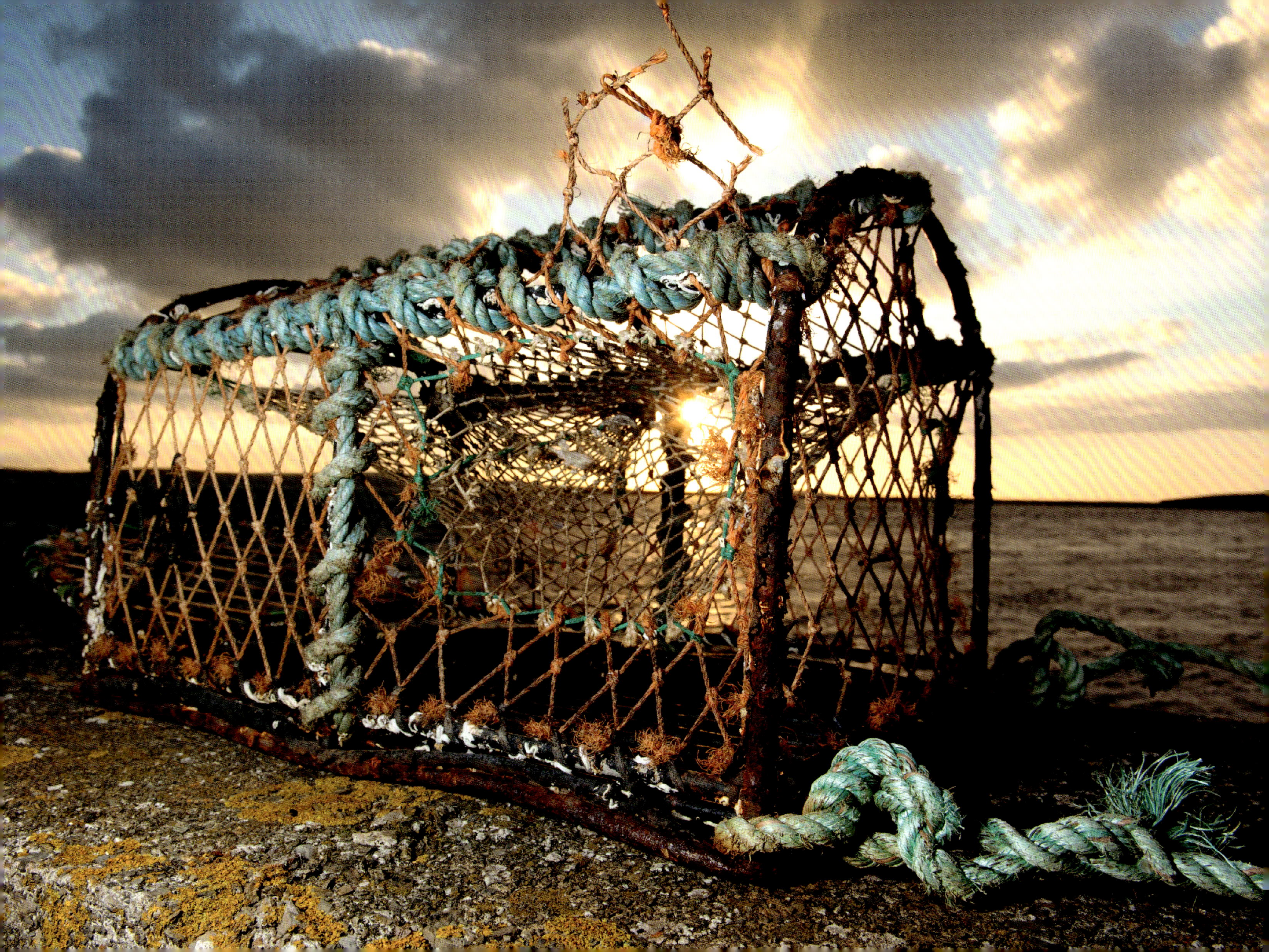

15 Fishing heritage

On a visit to Orkney in 1814 the writer Sir Walter Scott remarked: *"The Orcadians seem by no means an alert or active race; they neglect the excellent fisheries which lie under their very noses…"*. Orkney was predominantly a farming community – fish were caught using long lines from boats for food and for oil for lamps, but not for sale.

In 1790 live lobsters began to be sold to London traders who carried them to the fish market at Billingsgate in tanks of seawater in the hold of their smacks. Thousands of live lobsters were taken to London from Orkney every week; many of them caught around Scapa Flow. The Thames Company (London) was the next to get involved, but this time it was cod that was on the menu. In 1817 the cod fisheries began in Orkney, centred on Burray where 11 sloops were based, rising to 18 sloops in 1840-42.

All this was nothing compared to what was to follow when the local lairds followed the example of the Dutch and fishing for herring started. The 'silver darlings' migrated around the coast of Britain during the year. In 1820 Herston, South Ronaldsay, was still an agricultural 'toonship' with no houses along the shore, but by 1827 the village had been built. By 1838, South Ronaldsay, with Herston and St Margaret's Hope, and the adjacent island of Burray, could boast 245 herring boats. Things were not all rosy, as small crofters in 19th century South Ronaldsay found their rent had been doubled by the laird in an attempt to force them to go to the fishing to earn extra money that would ultimately end up in his pocket.

In 1829 Alexander Sutherland Graeme proposed to build a fishing village on his estate in Holm. The first house was built the same year and leased to a cooper, whose skill was crucial for the new venture. By 1832 three houses had been built and in the following year it was first referred to as St Mary's.

Herring fishing was already in decline by the 1840s but in 1888 it re-emerged as a major industry. A huge herring fleet arrived every summer, accompanied by a large workforce of gutters and coopers. Stromness was an important centre, where wooden piers and accommodation huts were built at the Point of Ness. Eventually the herring population crashed through over-fishing, but the industry in St Mary's, Burray and South Ronaldsay was effectively finished off by the sinking of blockships and later by the building of the Barriers, which cut them off from their fishing grounds.

The herring fishing fleet leaving Stromness.
(Orkney Library & Archive)

A *'Fifie'* herring boat at St Mary's, Holm. The *'Fifie'* has a vertical bow and stern.
(Orkney Library & Archive)

The herring curing station at Burray Village, now the Sands Hotel.
(Orkney Library & Archive)

'Zulu' herring boats at Burray Village. The *'Zulu'* has a vertical bow and sloping 'raked' stern.
(Orkney Library & Archive)

A *'Fifie'* herring boat at St Margaret's Hope, South Ronaldsay.
(Orkney Library & Archive)

Herring boats returning to Stromness; note the number of boats tied up all along the seafront.
(Orkney Library & Archive)

An old ship's anchor lies beside the 17th century store house at St Mary's, Holm.
(Drew Kennedy)

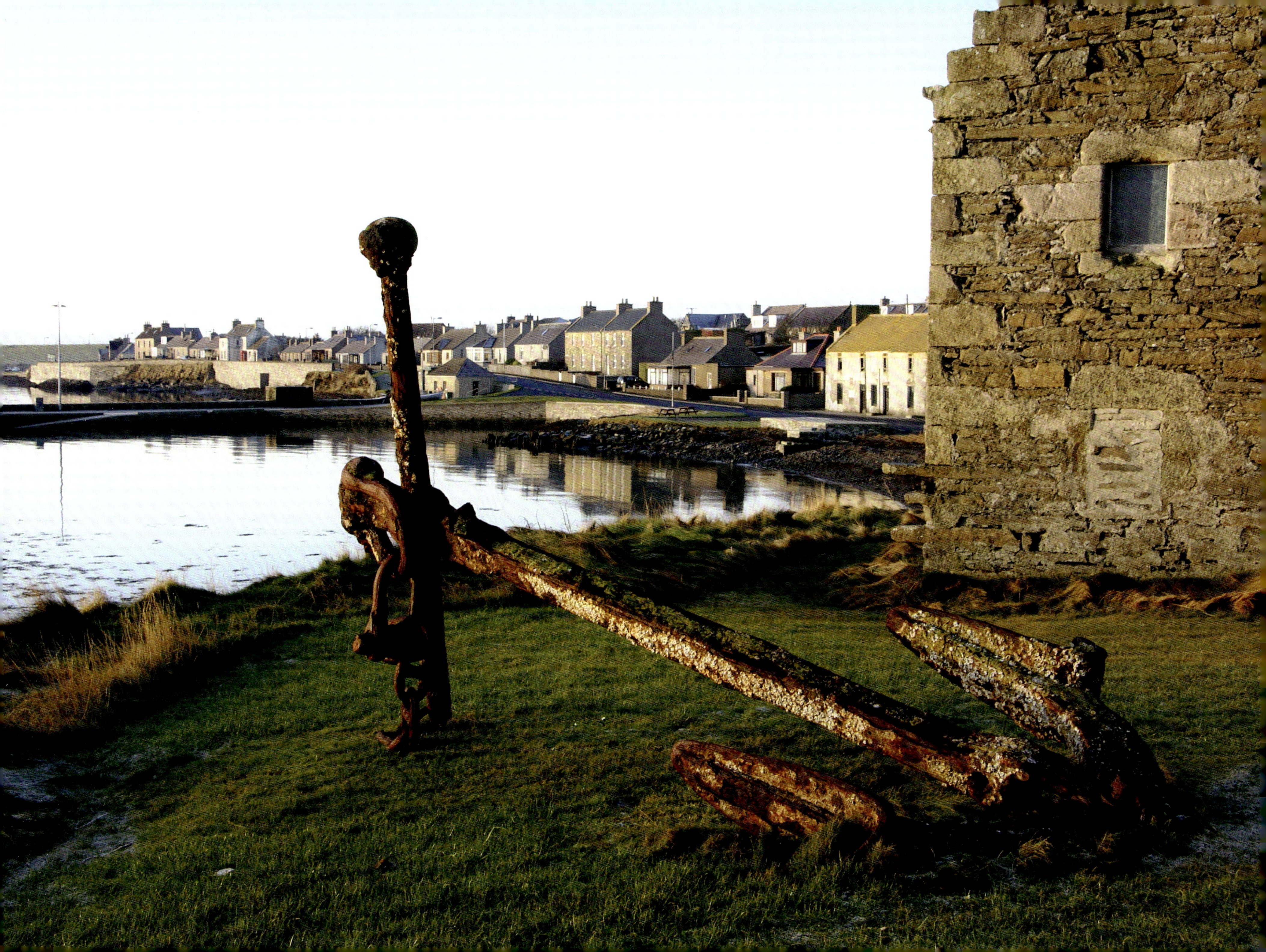

One of Northern Lighthouse Board's minor lights sits on the Barrel of Butter. (SFLPS)

Common Seal underwater at the Barrel of Butter. (Ian Potten)

With this silhouette, it can just about be understood how the Barrel of Butter can be mistaken for a submarine in poor visibility. (Kevin Heath)

16 The Barrel of Butter

A small skerry called the Barrel of Butter lies to the northeast of Cava and has a strange story attached to it. It was said that when St Magnus Cathedral was being built in Kirkwall, women would set off to walk to Hoy to fetch red sandstone for the building. They walked, magically, over the waters of Scapa Flow; back and fore, carrying the stones in their 'bratos' (a coarse apron). This went on for some time before the day came when there was enough stone for the building. When the women who were returning heard of this they all tipped their burden of stones into the sea at one spot, and that was how the Barrel of Butter was created.

The historian would be quick to point out that the red sandstone of the cathedral did not, in fact, come from Hoy at all; but this story may not be what it seems. The Barrel of Butter is a relatively new name for this skerry; the original name was the Carlin Skerry. The Old Norse word *'Kerling'* was a derogatory term for an old woman, meaning old hag or witch. Witches in Orkney had a reputation for causing shipwreck through raising storms or sea fog, so maybe the old belief was that this dangerous rock was created by witches as a danger to shipping. A 6m tall beacon was built on it in 1853, with a light added in 1980. During World War II it was shelled by a ship that mistook it for a submarine.

The Barrel of Butter derives its current name from the annual rent that was paid for it. The sea never completely covers the skerry. The rocks are a popular haul out for both Common Seals and the larger Grey Seals. A seal fishery was based on this rock. This was mostly for the blubber, which was rendered down into oil for lamps, but also for the skin and meat (although it was only the poorest people who ate seal). A farmer from Orphir paid the laird a barrel of seal oil every year for the right to hunt there. An increase in shipping was blamed for driving the seals away from the skerry. The laird was reluctant to lose his annual rent from the rock, but it was reduced to a barrel of butter, hence the name.

In Orkney folklore seals, or selkies as they are known, were thought to be the souls of people who had drowned, condemned to swim in the ocean as seals. At certain times of the year these selkie folk could take off their skins and dance at night in human form, but had to be back in the water by sunrise. There are stories of men who fell in love with selkie maidens and stole their skins, forcing them to live on land until such time that they could recover their missing skins and return to the deep. It was only the Grey Seal that had the power to transform, not the Common Seal.

◀ Intrepid explorers are greeted by a fly-past of Purple Sandpipers on the Barrel of Butter in winter. (SFLPS)

The Barrel of Butter with Flotta beyond. (Dmitry Rostophin) ▶

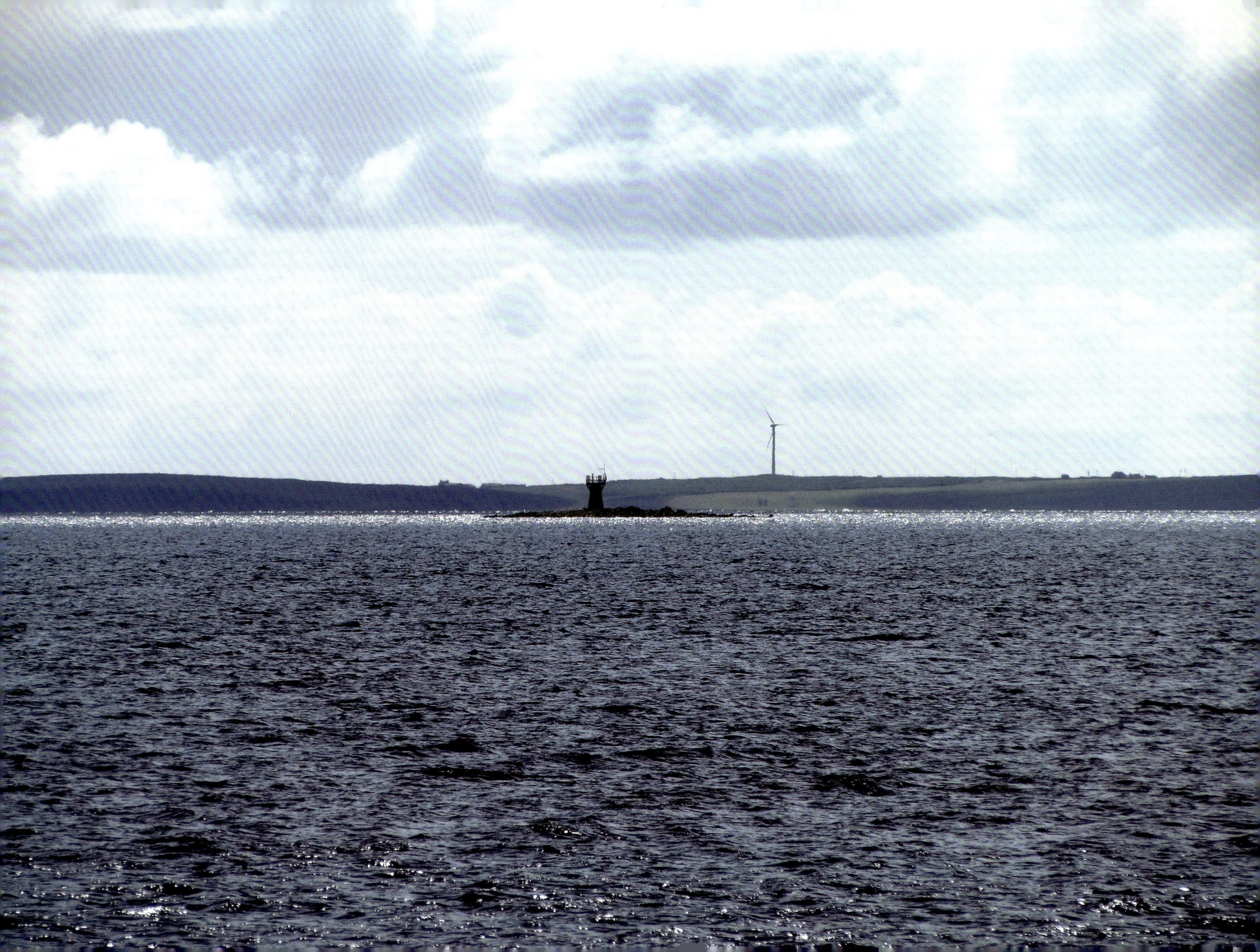

Construction of the huge oil tanks at Flotta. (Orkney Library & Archive)

'The Flotta Jotter', the newsletter produced during the construction of the Flotta Oil Terminal. (Orkney Library & Archive)

Tony Benn, Energy Secretary (front left) and Dr Armand Hammer (centre) at the opening of the Flotta Oil Terminal. (Orkney Library & Archive)

17 Oil

In January 1973 Occidental Oil (UK) Ltd announced the discovery of the Piper Oil Field in the North Sea, 100 miles east of Wick, followed by the Claymore field in 1974. Flotta was selected as the site for the oil terminal that was estimated to cost £25 million to build (the final bill was actually £100 million). Work began in early 1974; the largest building project seen in Scapa Flow in peacetime. The construction workforce included, among others, hundreds of Irish workmen and for a while there was a twice weekly direct flight between Kirkwall and Belfast. The first oil flowed from the Piper Field on 7 December 1976, but it took 20 days to fill the 130 mile long pipeline that snaked across the seabed, passing under the road just beyond No. 4 Barrier in South Ronaldsay, before arriving at Flotta. The iconic symbol of the oil industry in Orkney, the Flotta Flare, was first lit at 02.00 hours on Tuesday 28 December 1976 to burn off excess gas. The terminal was officially opened on 11 January 1977 by the Energy Secretary, Tony Benn MP, and Occidental's Chairman Dr Armand Hammer.

Since then it has twice passed into other ownership – to Elf in 1991 and to Talisman Energy in 2000. Once the crude oil reaches Flotta, impurities, salt water and hydrocarbon gasses are removed before it is shipped out by tanker. Oil tankers can berth at the jetty and take on oil or liquid gas while larger tankers can use one of the two Single Point Moorings situated out to sea (although only one of them is currently in use).

Since 1980 ship-to-ship transfer of oil has taken place, allowing huge tankers to be used. In 2007 the world's first

The *Dolabella* was the first tanker to be loaded with oil from Flotta on 11 January 1977. (Orkney Library & Archive)

Flotta Oil Terminal under construction. (Orkney Library & Archive)

ship to ship transfer of liquid natural gas took place here. The oil industry also supports the pilot boats and tugs used to guide tankers into Scapa Flow and berth them.

On July 6 1988 the Piper Alpha oil platform was destroyed in a series of explosions, with 167 lives lost in the inferno. The 1,100 tonne accommodation module, where many of the victims' bodies lay, was lifted from the seabed and set on a barge and brought into Scapa Flow. Here, away from the prying eyes of the media, Grampian Police began the grim task of recovering and identifying bodies in an operation that lasted four months.

A ship-to-ship transfer of oil in Scapa Flow. (Orkney Photographic)

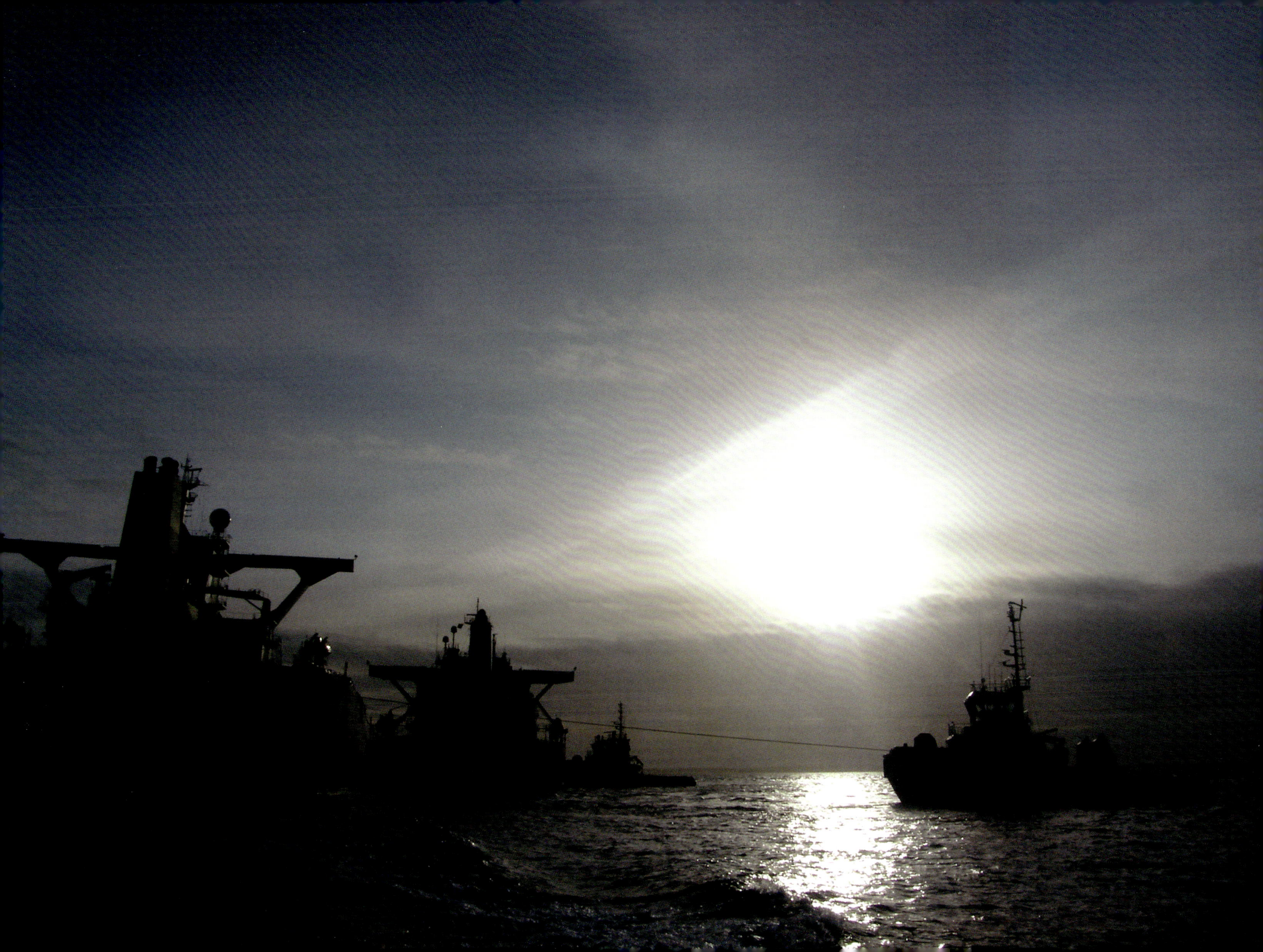

The EMEC test support buoy deployed at their scale wave test site off Howequoy Head in Scapa Flow. The scale test site provides the opportunity for prototype wave energy technologies to undergo sea trials in more gentle conditions. (Mike Brookes-Roper, courtesy of EMEC)

18 Renewable energy

The old naval base at Lyness is all set to play a new role as a centre for the renewable energy industry following £3 million of Orkney Islands Council investment. Phase 1 of the Lyness development refaced the old World War II 'Golden Wharf' to give 265 metres of mooring for ships. The site will be used for storing, assembling and servicing marine renewable energy devices, which will be tested in Orkney waters. There is already a full scale marine energy test site run by EMEC (the European Marine Energy Centre) at Billia Croo off Outertown, Stromness, where wave energy devices are tested. Pelamis Wave Power of Leith has already set up a base at Lyness. Phase 2 will see large buildings along the wharf and it is hoped that Lyness will become a centre for research in marine renewable energy as well as providing support for nearby test sites.

When a 900Kw wind turbine in Burray started to generate electricity in February 2005, it made history by being the first locally-owned grid-connected wind generator in Scotland. It is run by Orkney Renewable Energy Ltd, a consortium of Orkney businesses, and supports a community investment fund distributed locally each year. It has an annual income in excess of £200,000 and has led the way for communities to invest in their own wind turbines.

In November 2010, Hoy took charge of its own community turbine, which had been delivered by ship to the Golden Wharf. The building of it necessitated the construction of 300m of road using 1,800 tonnes of rock with 17.5 tonnes of reinforcing steel and 400 tonnes of concrete for the foundations of the turbine and substation. It went into service in October 2011, being delayed because a turbine part was to be supplied by a Japanese factory which had been destroyed by the terrible earthquake and tsunami.

The wind turbine in Flotta was operational by June 2010. It is run by a Stromness-based business, and has caused a stir on the island, but expects to give £100,000 to the Flotta community during the turbine's working life. A further Orkney business currently has plans to build a wind farm on Fara, which could prove even more controversial.

Pelamis Sea Snake tidal energy device being towed through Scapa Flow. (Orkney Photographic)

Divers in action at an EMEC test site. (Mike Brookes-Roper, courtesy of EMEC)

Looking from South Ronaldsay to Flotta. (Raymond Besant)

The Burray wind turbine. (Rebecca Marr)

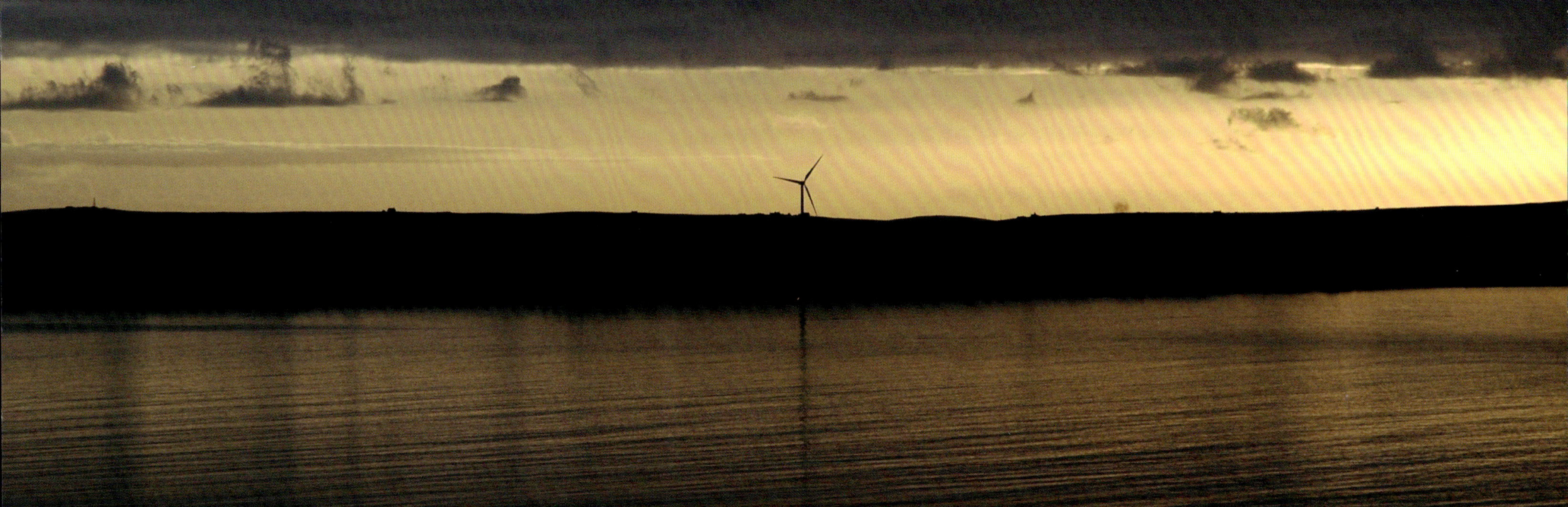

19 The Orkney Folk Festival

regular visitor to the Festival enjoys the atmosphere in the Royal Hotel, Stromness. (Orkney Photographic)

Session at the Ferry Inn, 2004. (Louis Decarlo for Orkney Folk Festival)

P.M. and Fiona Driver at the Pier Head, Stromness. (Louis Decarlo for Orkney Folk Festival)

In the early 1980s, Orkney Tourist Board's Chief Executive, Josh Gourlay, was watching the development of festivals in other areas with interest. He had supported the St Magnus Festival when it began in 1977 and was keen to see festivals becoming part of the island calendar. Discussions about a folk festival started with Shetland Tourist Board, as there were concerns that traditional music was on the decline. Howie Firth, the producer of BBC Radio Orkney, also played an active role in the creation of the festival. Things came to a head in 1982 when Marjory Linklater, widow of the Orkney writer Eric Linklater, needed funding to invite the Northern Irish poet James Simmons to Orkney. Howie offered sponsorship through Radio Orkney if a package could be put together involving musicians as well as the poet. Paul Muldoon, a BBC producer in Northern Ireland (and a renowned poet) found the funding and the event went ahead.

The Scottish Arts Council could provide funding to an official organisation and so the Orkney Folk Festival Society was formed. For 25 years Johnny Mowat was the Chair of the festival, ably assisted in the beginning by local fiddle player Len Wilson. The new society met for the first time at the end of December 1982 to plan a festival that would be based in Stromness and held at the end of May 1983. From modest beginnings the Orkney Folk Festival has grown in size and stature over the years, winning 'Event of the Year' in the MG Alba Traditional Music Awards in 2011.

It is true to say that the Folk Festival has been the catalyst in reviving the fortunes of traditional music in Orkney. The 'Open Stage' event has launched the careers of many

The leaflet for the first Orkney Folk Festival in 1983. (Orkney Library & Archive)

musicians as the winner gets a chance to compete in the huge Celtic Connections Festival in Glasgow. Music tutor Douglas Montgomery has taken the Kirkwall Grammar School group Hadhirgaan to Canada twice. But it is Stromness that is the home of the Orkney Folk Festival and in the last weekend in May the town is packed with musicians and there is a real carnival atmosphere. Apart from the ticketed concerts there are pub sessions in every bar, and on nice days this spills over into the streets where the music plays long into the night.

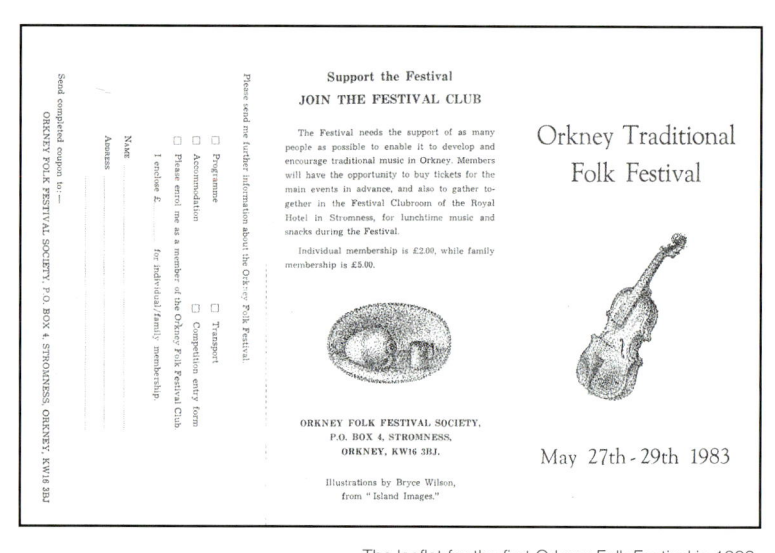

◀ Birsay Boys Sunday Session in the Royal Hotel, Stromness. (Colin Keldie)

Laura Beth Salter from The Shee with her mandolin in the Upstairs Bar of the Stromness Hotel. (Rebecca Marr) ▶

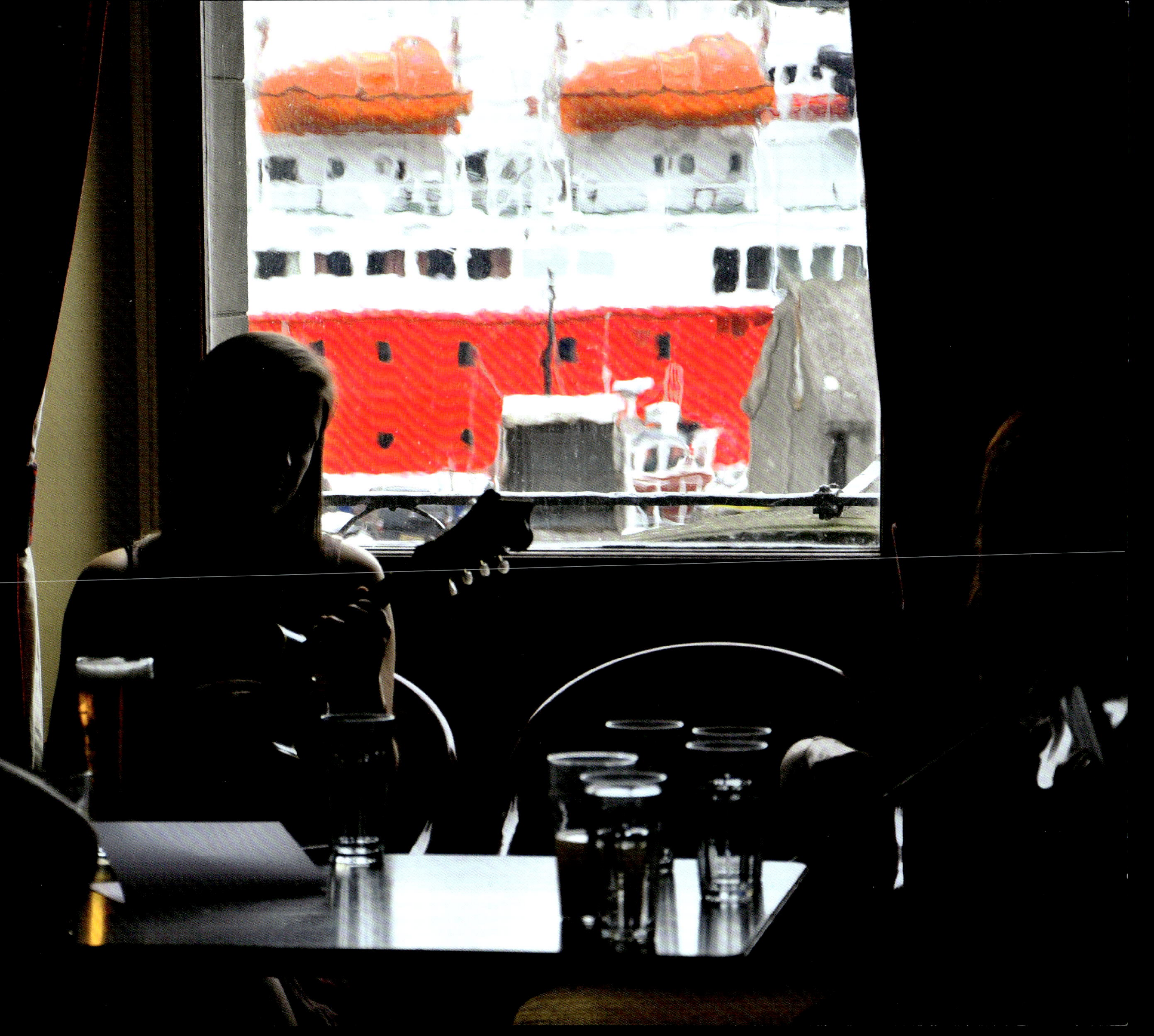

20 The South Ronaldsay Boys' Ploughing Match

Boys' Ploughing Match, Burray.
(Orkney Library & Archive)

Boys' Ploughing Match, South Ronaldsay.
(Orkney Library & Archive)

Great excitement at the Boys' Ploughing Match, South Ronaldsay.
(Orkney Library & Archive)

Horses and ploughs, South Ronaldsay.
(Orkney Library & Archive)

The South Ronaldsay Boys' Ploughing Match and the Festival of the Horse are now a unique event in the Orkney calendar; a celebration of the days when horsepower dominated the farm. It is now held on the third Saturday in August in the village of St Margaret's Hope and at the nearby Sands o' Wright. Here the boys gather with miniature ploughs, either of wood or metal, to compete against each other in a trial of farming skill.

The origin of the event is unknown, but it seems to have had humble beginnings. Originally the ploughs were not the finely crafted family heirlooms of today, but crude and simple representations of a plough made from a cow's hoof fastened to a stick. Local blacksmith Bill Hourston made the first miniature metal plough in the 1920s. The ploughing didn't take place on a beach either, but in a kale yard or potato patch, where the soil was very soft and loose. For many years it was held on the first Wednesday in April, at the same time as the adults were ploughing the land; obviously a case of the boys imitating their fathers. Why it became a competition is unknown, but it seems that the younger boys also wanted to join in, and so they started dressing up as horses with imitation harness.

It seems that similar ploughing matches were also held in other areas as well. One was recorded in Stronsay (where the small 'horse' pulled the ploughs) and in Burray, whilst in South Ronaldsay there were also competitions in the districts of Grimness and in Widewall, where it only ended with the closure of the local school in the 1960s.

The festival these days is based at the Cromarty Hall in St Margaret's Hope. Here the smaller children in their horse costumes are judged. It used to be a boys only affair until girls were admitted after World War II. Their costumes are enhanced by the addition of brooches, tinsel and anything shiny. They have a mane, tail and shaggy coverings over the feet, like a real Clydesdale horse. Their shoes even have a band of silver paint around the front, like a horseshoe. The action then moves to the beach where the ploughs are judged; wood and metal have their own categories. Lots are drawn for the 'flats', a four foot (1.22m) square patch of sand. They then have 45 minutes to plough it. There are three classes; Under 8, Ordinary and Champion. A committee judges the ploughing on straightness, best ends and neatest finish. After that they retire to the Cromarty Hall for tea.

Boys' Ploughing Match at the Sands o' Wright, South Ronaldsay.
(Orkney Photographic)

The Festival of the Horse, South Ronaldsay.
(Orkney Photographic)

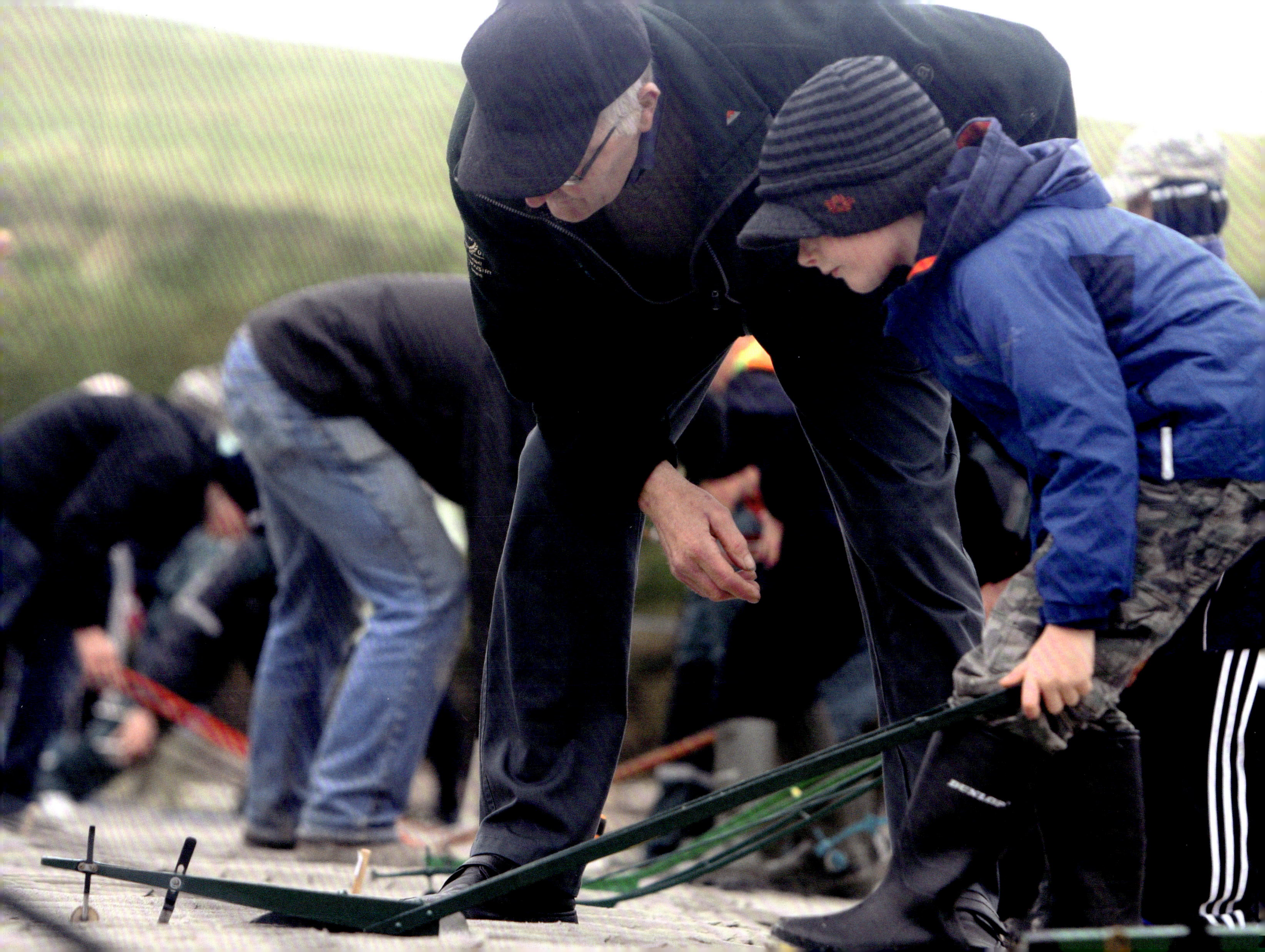

The Saltaire, the first Stromness Lifeboat, being launched at the slipway at the Point of Ness. (Orkney Library & Archive)

Coxswain Dan Kirkpatrick and the crew of the Longhope Lifeboat, Thomas McCunn, in the late 1950s; many of them were lost in the Longhope Lifeboat Disaster. L-R: (Back row) Dan Kirkpatrick, J. Johnston, R. Johnston, J. Norquoy, R. Kirkpatrick. (Front row) R. Johnston, R. Johnston, J. Nicolson. (Orkney Library & Archive)

The Longhope Lifeboat T.G.B. (Orkney Library & Archive)

21 Lifeboats

On New Year's Day 1866 the emigrant ship *Albion*, bound for America, was wrecked on the Point of Oxan, Graemsay, just below Hoy Low Lighthouse. She had been battered by a storm and driven towards Orkney, the crew too exhausted to prevent disaster. Most of the 100 passengers and crew were rescued by Graemsay men in their boats, although local man Joseph Mowat and 10 passengers were killed when his boat capsized. A call was made for a lifeboat to be stationed at Stromness. The following year the *Saltaire* went into service, paid for by the Bradford industrialist and philanthropist Titus Salt and stationed at the Point of Ness on Hoy Sound.

The dangerous waters of the Pentland Firth have claimed many ships. In 1874 it was decided to station the lifeboat, *Dickinson Edleston*, at Brims in Longhope. Like Stromness, the Longhope Lifeboat is still in service and saving lives. On the evening of Monday 17 March 1969 a distress call from the stricken Liberian registered ship SS *Irene* saw the launch of the Longhope Lifeboat, *T.G.B.*, under the command of Coxswain Dan Kirkpatrick. Dan was a legend in the RNLI, having been awarded the silver medal for gallantry three times and even featuring in the popular TV show 'This Is Your Life'.

The weather conditions were atrocious, but lives were in danger and the lifeboat heeded the call. The new Kirkwall Lifeboat, *Grace Patterson Ritchie*, joined in the rescue, reporting mountainous waves 60 feet (18m) high, described at the time as being like "a liquid cliff". The last sighting of the *TGB* was by the Principal Keeper at Cantick Head Lighthouse who saw her lights a mile east

◀ *The wreck of the Irene at Grim Ness, South Ronaldsay. The Longhope Lifeboat T.G.B. was lost attempting to help her. (Orkney Library & Archive)*

An aerial view of the wreck of the Irene. (Orkney Library & Archive)

of him at 9.35 pm. The *Irene*, which had run out of fuel and seemed to have no idea of its location, was driven ashore at Grim Ness, South Ronaldsay and the crew was rescued by the Deerness Rocket Brigade who took them off by breeches buoy. The loss of radio contact with the *T.G.B.* led to a full scale search which ended when the Thurso Lifeboat found her upturned hull four miles south-west of Tor Ness, Walls. Her eight man crew were all dead; a tragic blow to the small community of Brims. Those lost were Dan Kirkpatrick and his two sons Daniel (Ray) and John (Jack), Robert Johnston and his two sons Jimmy and Robert, Eric McFadyen and James Swanson (whose body was never found). A bronze statue of a lifeboat man by North Ronaldsay artist Ian Scott was unveiled by Queen Elizabeth the Queen Mother on 9 August 1970. The coxswain of the current Longhope Lifeboat, *Helen Comrie*, is Kevin Kirkpatrick, Dan's grandson.

The Longhope Lifeboat Shed at Brims. It is now a museum and houses the beautifully restored Longhope Lifeboat Thomas McCunn (1933-62). (Rebecca Marr) ▶

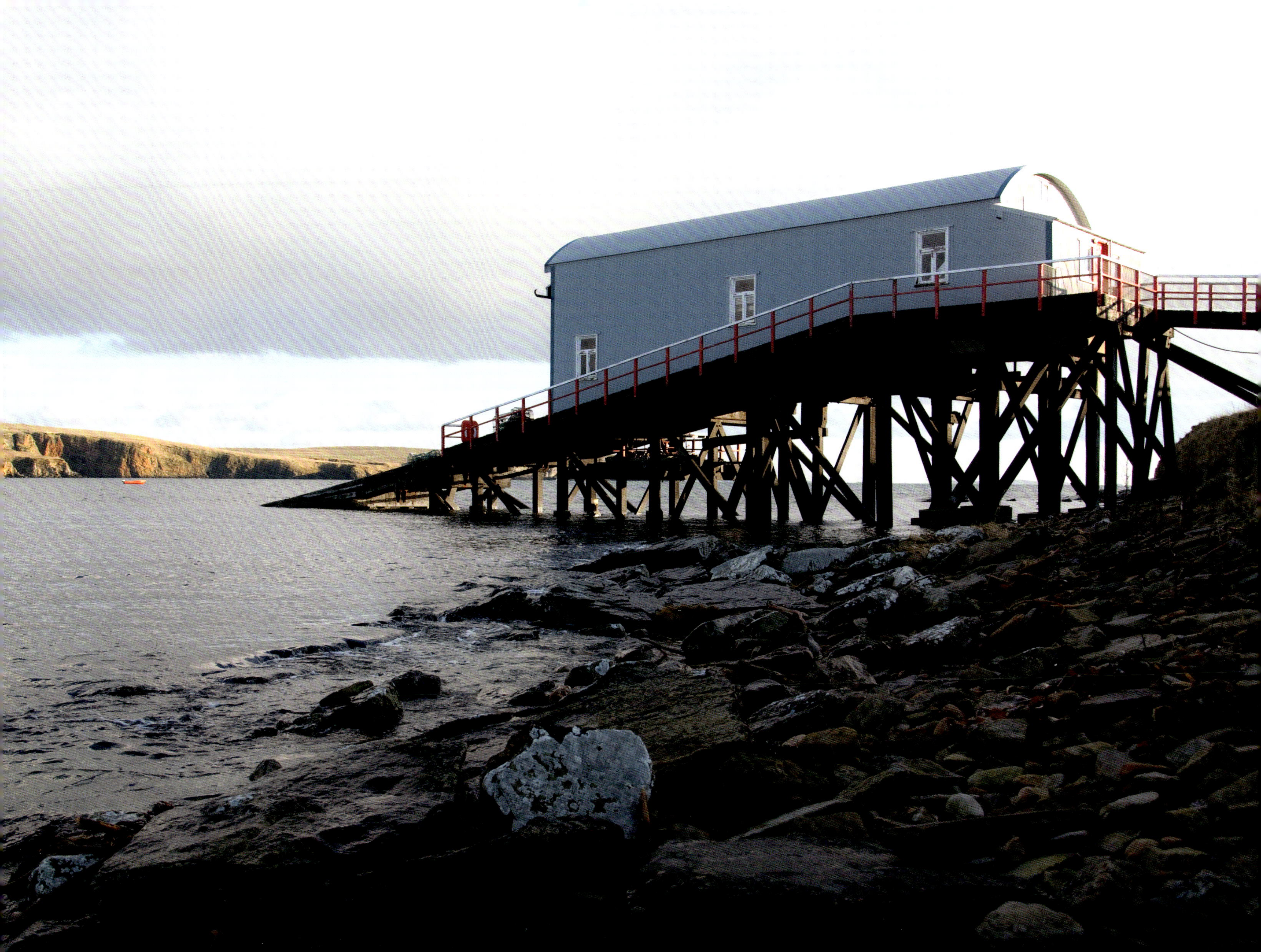

22 Ferries

When the railway reached Thurso in 1874, Highland Railways successfully lobbied the government to grant them the passenger and mail contract to Orkney. In 1880 Scapa Pier was built, and for a short time it was the terminal for the mail to the islands before the Railways withdrew in 1882 and the North Company took over. Several ferries had served the islands of Hoy, Graemsay, Cava, Fara and Flotta, including the South Isles Steam Packet Company, who had a new vessel, *Saga*, built at Copland's Dock in Stromness in 1893. Their service proved to be unreliable, through poor management, and they went into liquidation in 1895. The Kirkwall merchant Robert Garden introduced his steamer *Hoy Head* to the route in 1896; she would serve under six different owners right up to 1956. St Margaret's Hope was later included in the service, which carried passengers, cargo and the mail. Garden already had a fleet of shop boats which sailed around Orkney and further afield selling groceries, animal feeds and even clothes, which could either be bought or bartered for fish, lobsters and eggs.

Both World Wars saw hundreds of thousands of service men and women travelling back and forth from Orkney. They arrived in Thurso on the 'Jellicoe Special', a train that ran from London's Euston Station and was named after the Commander-in-Chief of the Grand Fleet. The steamers *St Ola* and *St Ninian* carried them on the final leg of their journey from Scrabster to Orkney during World War I.

In World War II the *St Ola* was joined by the *Earl of Zetland* on the Stromness route while the *St Ninian* carried sailors direct to Lyness. The Navy ran an excellent two-hourly ferry service during World War II, which was also available to civilians. The routes were Lyness - Scapa Pier; Lyness - Longhope; Lyness - Fara - Cava; Lyness - Houton - Stromness - Flotta - St Margaret's Hope. This continued after the war until the final route, a twice daily service from Lyness - Houton, was stopped when the Naval Base at Lyness closed in 1957. Bremner and Co. were the last independent ferry operators to the South Isles, taken over in 1973 by Orkney Islands Shipping Company (now Orkney Ferries). The roll-on, roll-off ferries *Hoy Head* and *Thorsvoe* now sail from Houton to Lyness, Longhope and Flotta, while the foot passenger ferry *Graemsay* sails from Stromness to Graemsay and Moaness on Hoy.

The South Isles steamer *Hoy Head*.
(Orkney Library & Archive)

The South Isles steamer *Suters*.
(Orkney Library & Archive)

The *St Ola* at Scapa Pier.
(Orkney Library & Archive)

The *Watchful* was a government sponsored vessel that went into service in 1961 for Bremner and Co.
(Orkney Library & Archive)

The NorthLink ferry *Hamnavoe* arriving in Stromness. The floating crane in the foreground was used at the experimental wave energy test site at Billia Croo.
(Rebecca Marr)

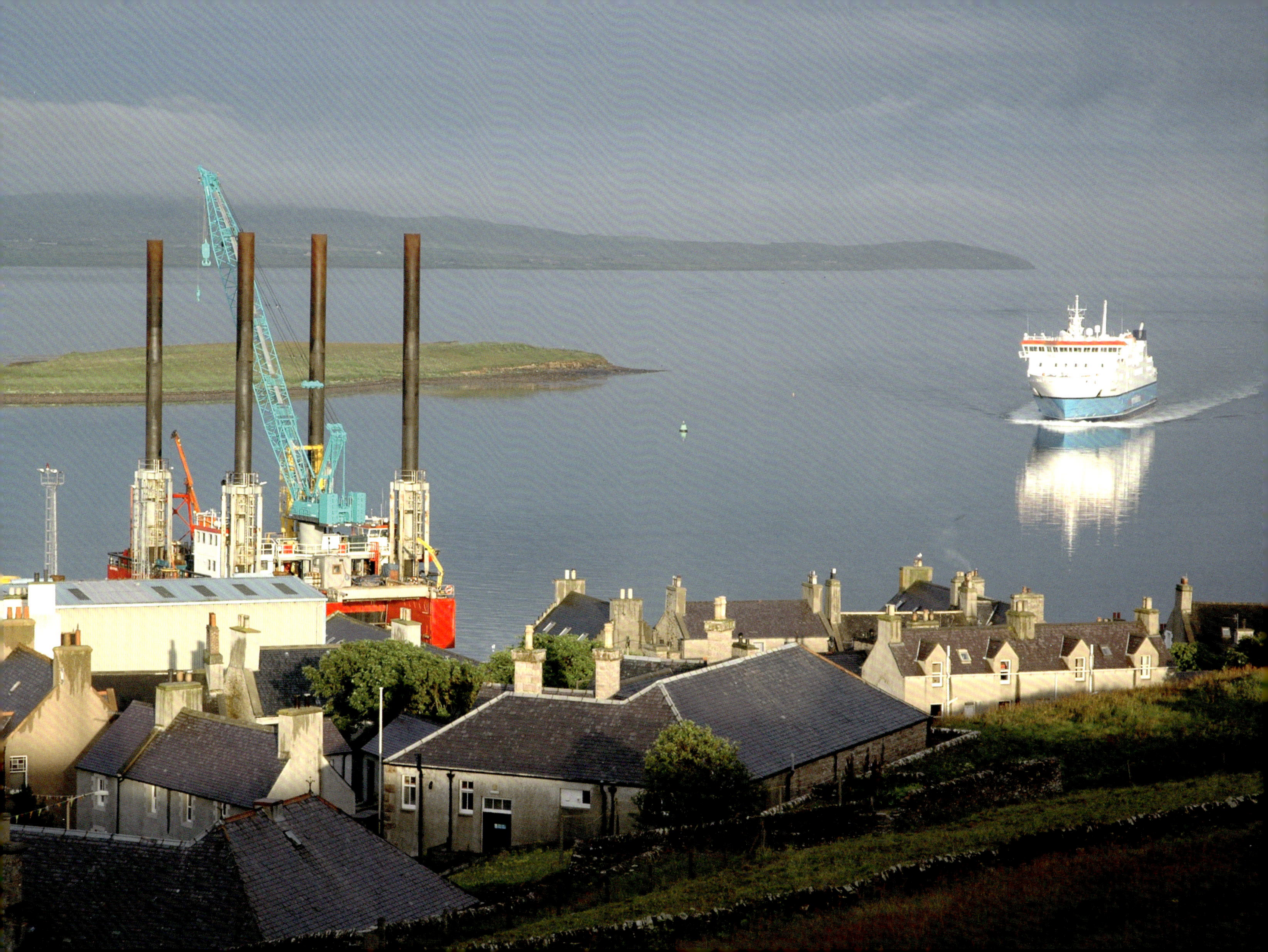

23 Diving

Scapa Flow is well-known worldwide as a 'must see' diving experience with diving bringing around £3 million a year into the local economy. The huge wrecks of the German High Seas Fleet, although damaged by salvage work and the ravages of time, are still highly impressive sights, while the four huge gun turrets from SMS *Bayern*, which were torn off during salvage work in 1934, also make a popular dive. It is not just the German ships that are on offer, as the blockships and a range of other wrecks also make fascinating dives.

The unsung hero of the diving industry is not actually a diver, but a museum curator. Bryce Wilson began setting up exhibitions at Stromness Museum in the early 1970s. At this time it was only just over 30 years since the last German Battlecruiser had been raised and salvage work was still going on at the remaining German ships, as well as HMS *Vanguard*. Bryce created the exhibition 'The Salving of the German Fleet' and a visit to the museum by Dutch historian Dan van der Vat led him to write the book 'The Grand Scuttle', which brought the story to a wider audience. More divers wanted to see these amazing wrecks for themselves, so dive boat operators set up in business to cater for them, led by John Thornton, Kirkwall and Anthony Duncan, Burray. As the numbers grew so did the risk of divers getting into trouble from decompression sickness so there is a hyperbaric chamber based at the Old Stromness Academy. The remaining wrecks have all been scheduled as Ancient Monuments and enjoy the same protection as sites like Skara Brae.

Salvage divers in Scapa Flow. (Orkney Library & Archive)

Salvage divers in Scapa Flow. (Orkney Library & Archive)

Salvage divers in Scapa Flow. (Orkney Library & Archive)

Nowadays divers treat the wrecks with respect, but this was not always the case. One example from the early 1970s was the brass letters from the name HMS *Royal Oak*, which one diver from the South of England spent his holiday tearing off the prohibited wreck. On his last dive he was having difficulty removing the letter 'A' and eventually forced it free, bending one leg of the letter in the process, only to drop it and lose it. The following year a friend of his was instructed to look for it, and found it, sending a telegram saying "A OK". The diver emigrated to Canada, taking the name plate with him. He jumbled up the letters and had them displayed on his wall. An elderly woman who visited said "That's Royal Oak". "How did you know?" he asked, to which she replied "I lost a brother on that ship." His conscience pricked, he handed the sign over to the Canadian Navy who returned it to the Admiralty, who presented it to the Scapa Flow Visitor Centre & Museum, Lyness.

A diver visiting the wreck of the SMS *Brummer*. (Gareth Lock) ▶

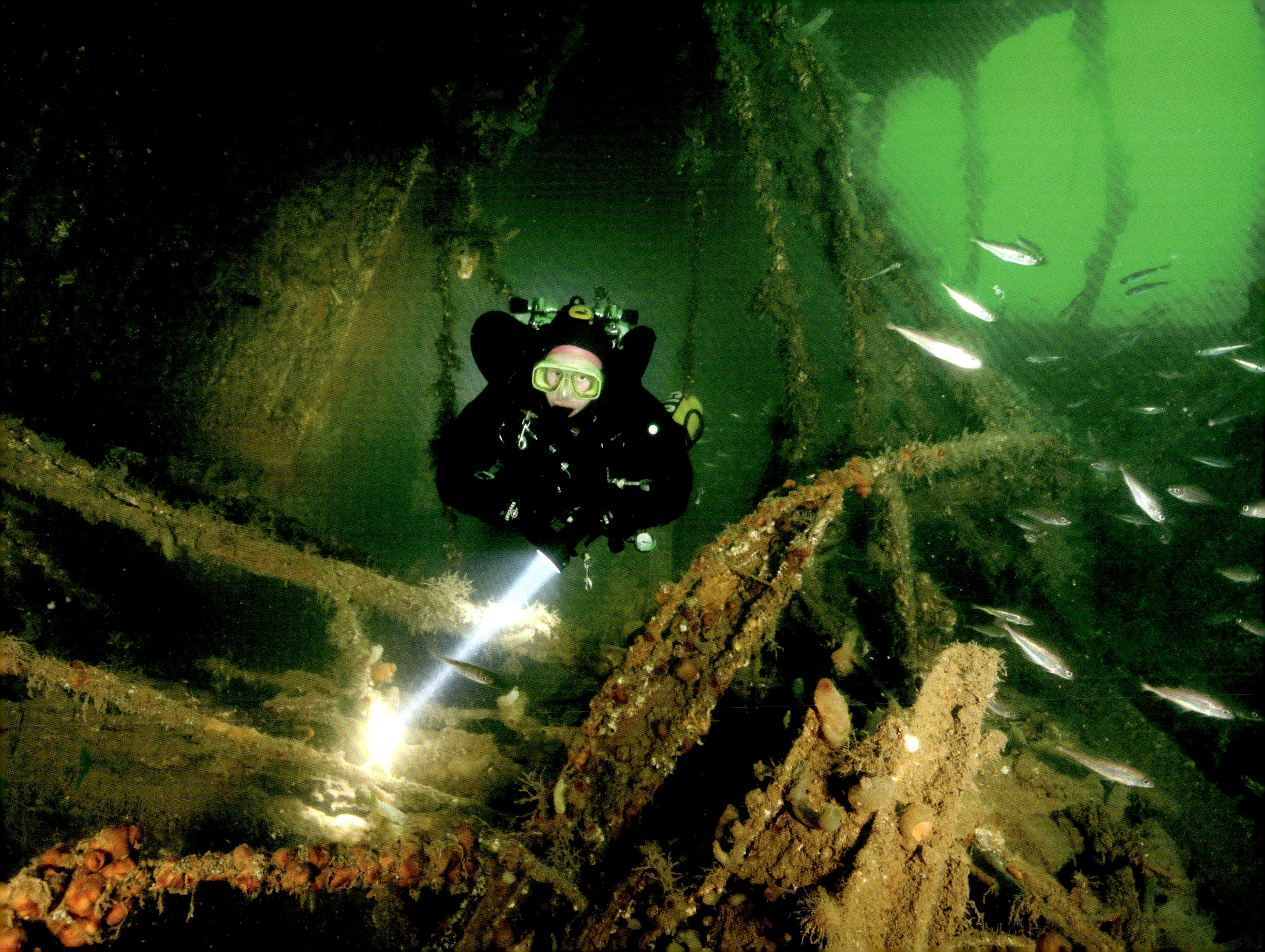

24 Island depopulation

The smaller Scapa Flow islands are now uninhabited, but they once supported communities of farmers and fishermen. While life for most of the inhabitants was uneventful, this was not always the case. On 10 June 1694 two French privateers (licensed pirates) landed on Lamb Holm and laid waste to the farm there, slaughtering or carrying off farm animals and destroying the crops in the field as well as all the household goods.

In 1725 John Gow, the Orkney pirate, carried out a raid on the island of Cava, an island that was always sparsely populated. There are two versions of what happened. One says that three women from Cava were carried off and so badly used by Gow and his men that when they were dumped back on the island's shore one of them died where she lay. The version given in the Old Statistical Account of 1795 by Rev Liddle is very different. In it he says Gow's men *"…carried off two young women from the island; and after keeping them for some days aboard their ship, returned them to their friends, loaded with presents; and they both soon afterwards got husbands."* Cava was finally abandoned in the 1940s, until two ladies, Ida Woodham and Meg Peckham, set up home on the island and lived there for 27 years, leaving in 1993.

During World War II there was an influx of servicemen to many of these islands, living in wooden huts and manning anti-aircraft batteries and barrage balloon sites. Equipment and personnel were moved south towards the end of the war, with huts from Scapa Flow reused in France after the D-Day landings.

The story of Fara is similar to that of Cava, and also mirrors that of many other of Orkney's small isles. In 1891 Fara had a population of 76 people living in 15 households. By the time that Bruce Tulloch wrote the entry for Walls and Flotta in the 3rd Statistical Account in 1951 the population was down to *"15 or 16"* and the schoolchildren had to attend the Walls School, only getting home at weekends. Tulloch predicted the inevitable fate of Fara when he concludes *"…it seems that it is only a question of time before it ceases to be inhabited."* In 1957 the only resident to have a telephone left the island, resulting in the erection of a telephone box with the number Fara 1. One of the five remaining inhabitants bought the island from the Melsetter estate for £600. The island was finally abandoned in 1965 and sold the following year to a grouse shooting group for £2,300.

Crop marks on Cava. (Rebecca Marr)

Shop boat visiting Cava. (Orkney Library & Archive)

Mr Kinmond, who lived on Cava in the early 20th Century. (Orkney Library & Archive)

Barrage balloon on Fara in World War II. (Orkney Library & Archive)

Ruin on Fara with a rusty neep chopper. (Anne Bignall/SFLPS)

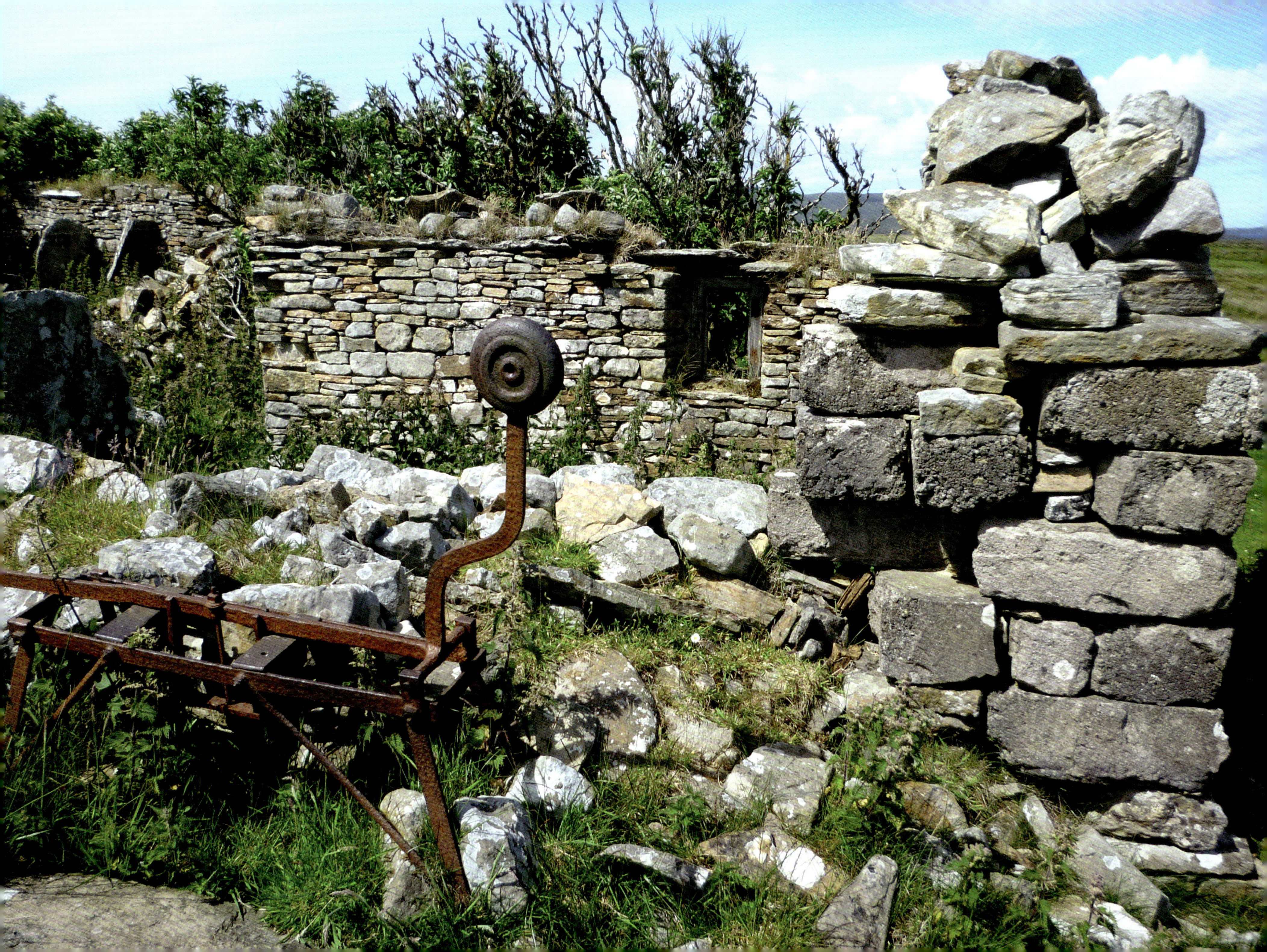

natural landscapes

Risso's Dolphins in Scapa Flow, between No. 1 Barrier and Holm pier. (Drew Kennedy)

25 Geology

The oldest rocks in Orkney are pinkish granite-gneiss and date from the Precambrian period, around 950 million years ago. These rocks are found at Stromness and Graemsay. They lay buried until around 500 million years ago when they were thrust upwards by the collision of continental landmasses.

Most of Orkney's rocks are termed Old Red Sandstone or Flagstones. They were formed during the Middle Devonian Period, around 380 million years ago. At this time the area that would one day become Orkney was part of an expanse of low-lying land to the south of the equator – the Orcadian Basin.

During wet periods the Orcadian Basin was filled with water that flowed in from the rivers that were fed by rainwater draining from the mountains, creating 'Lake Orcadie'. In dry periods, evaporation left a desert with a number of small saline lakes remaining in the lowest points.

The rivers that flowed into the lake brought mud and sand with them, laying down layer upon layer of sediments that gives Orkney its flat, easily split flagstone. Later, around 250 million years ago during the Permian Period, uplift of the land caused splits to open in the Devonian rock, into which igneous rock from deep below the surface was forced, creating what is known as a 'trap dyke'. There are good examples all around Scapa Flow.

Lake Orcadie was not lifeless, as we can see from the fossil record. The West Shore in Stromness has a fossilised shoreline, as the early rocks that had been pushed upwards formed an island in Lake Orcadie – today's Brinkie's Brae. Sun cracks in the stone show where the lake had once dried out, while rain pits and ripple marks denote wet periods. Around the West Shore can be found the fossil remains of Stromatolites – mats of algae, built up over decades – now called 'horse-tooth stone'.

Fossilised fish and plant remains can also be found in the stone that was once the deep lake bed. Examples are on display in the Stromness Museum and the Orkney Fossil & Heritage Centre in Burray. The geologist Hugh Miller (1802-56) collected fossils in Orkney as part of his research, which in turn had an influence on the work of Charles Darwin.

Lower Eday Dune Sandstone exposed below Buchanan Battery, Flotta. (Rebecca Marr)

The irregular granite-gneiss blocks in this wall near Stromness highlight the underlying geology here, so different from the flagstone found over almost all of Orkney. (Rebecca Marr)

Fossil fish *Gyroptichius agassizi* from Lake Orcadie deposits, on display at the Orkney Fossil & Heritage Centre, Burray. (Rhona Jenkins)

Above and right: The cliffs of the Kame of Hoy show a clear succession from Upper Stromness Group Flagstones, with brown Volcanic Ash above, then dark grey Columnar Basalts and topped by the Hoy Sandstones. (Premysl Fojtu)

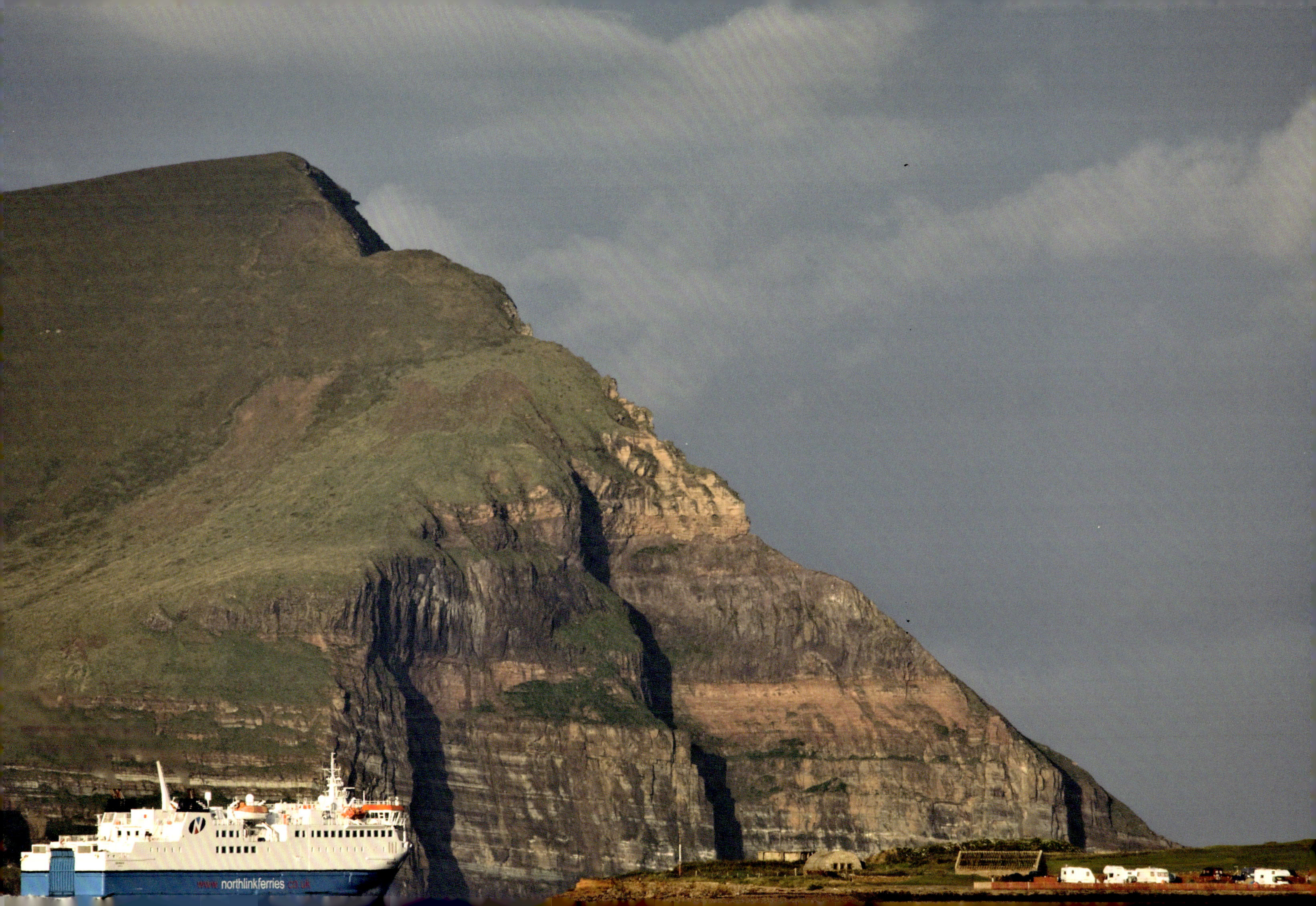
northlinkferries

26 The shaping of a landscape

Orkney's landscape has been sculpted by repeated glaciations. Around 850,000 years ago, early in the ice age, small glaciers formed on Hoy. By 100,000 years ago, during the last, Devensian, glaciation, Orkney was again covered with ice, which ground down the hills and formed wide U-shaped valleys. The ice sheets also carved out three large hollows, known as 'corries' (from the Gaelic word 'coire' meaning a pot or cauldron), into the Hills of Hoy. The ice sheets came and went over this period as temperatures varied, until the end of the last glaciation (around 12,000 years ago) when the sea level rose dramatically to separate Orkney from Scotland.

The first people to arrive in Orkney during the Mesolithic (Middle Stone Age), at least 9,000 years ago, would have found a very different landscape to that of today. The sea level was still rising, with land connecting Hoy with West Mainland. Scapa Flow was much smaller with a single entrance to the sea at Hoxa Sound.

Below the hilltops, woodland would have been widespread. At low spring tides the remains of prehistoric tree stumps can still be seen in sheltered bays around Scapa Flow. The decline of trees, triggered at least in part by human influence, combined with a cooler, wetter climate during the early Bronze Age, led to blanket bogs, dominated by *Sphagnum* mosses, building up across much of the landscape. The resulting peat has been cut for fuel in Orkney for thousands of years.

The absorbent and antiseptic qualities of *Sphagnum* would see the moss itself gathered in huge amounts to make field dressings for wounded soldiers in World War I.

Today, the peat deposits at Hobbister, overlooking Scapa Flow, are sustainably cut to supply the peat used in malting the barley, giving Highland Park whisky its smoky flavour.

Before the 1850s, the islands must have looked very brown and barren to the sailors entering Scapa Flow with much of the landscape covered by moorland. By the second half of the 19th century, agriculture was starting to become important to the landowners in the aftermath of the collapse of the lucrative kelp industry. Grants were available to drain wetlands and to reseed with clover. Orkney slowly started to turn green as land was reclaimed from low-lying areas to the hills.

Hoy Low Lighthouse framed by the flanks of Ward Hill, Hoy. (Rebecca Marr)

Greylag Geese in barley stubble on a coarse day, with Flotta in the murk beyond. (Raymond Besant)

The Howe at Dam of Hoxa, South Ronaldsay on a winter afternoon. (Raymond Besant)

Sheep on Hoy with Rysa Little in the foreground; Cava beyond; Wideford Hill and Keelylang in the distance. (Rebecca Marr)

Looking across a misty Clestrain Sound to the hills of Hoy. (Bill Jenman)

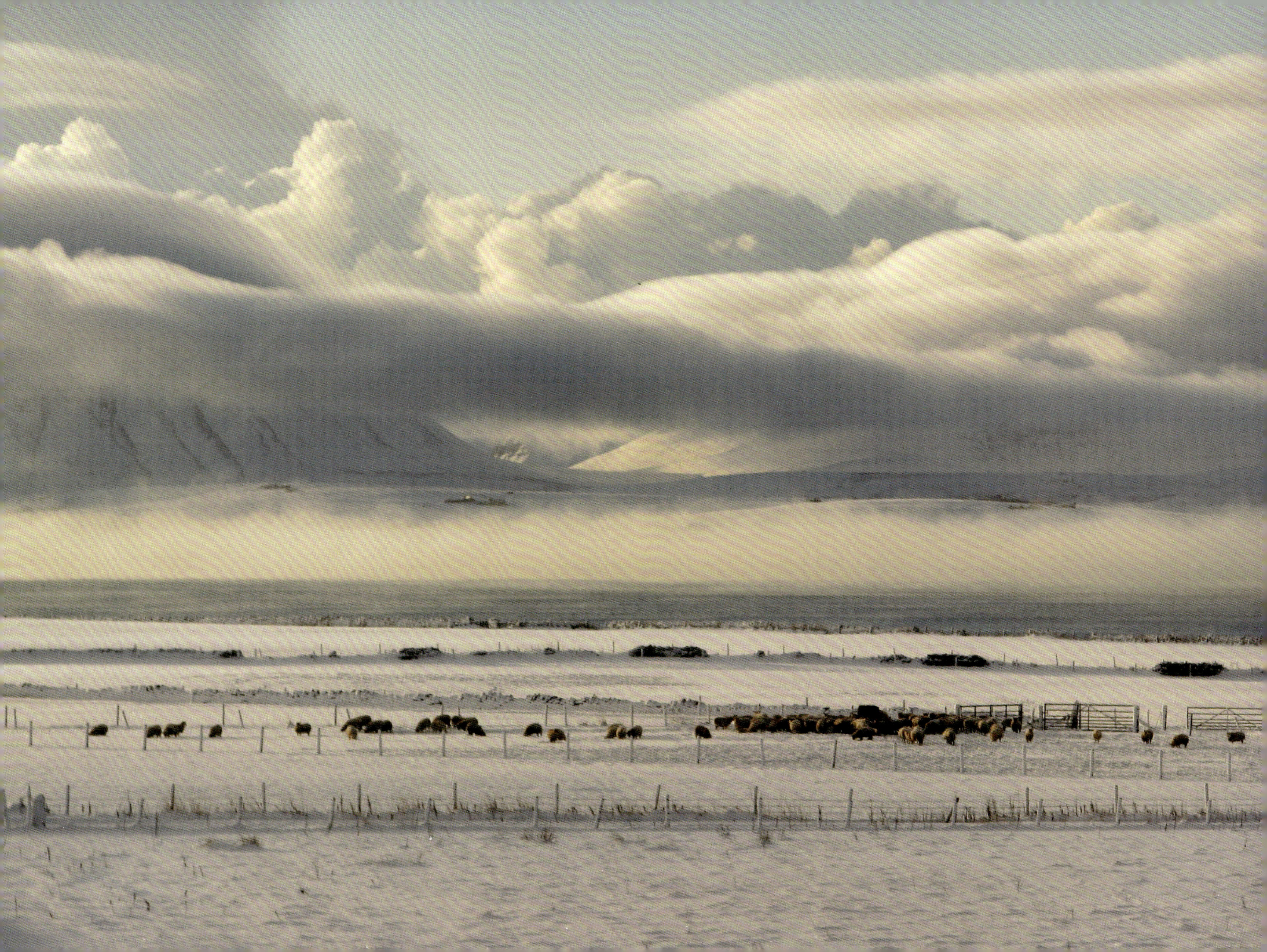

27 Echoes of woodland

At first glance, there is little in the way of trees around Scapa Flow, save for the conifer plantations on Flotta and Hoy. However, this initial appearance is misleading as sheltered spots provide a vital refuge for remnants of natural woodland. In addition, tiny Aspens are found on some exposed cliff tops, whilst Orkney's only native conifer, the Juniper, occurs sparsely as ground-hugging shrubs dotted around the cliff top and moor.

The largest, most intact ancient wood in Orkney survives at Berriedale, hidden amongst the Hoy hills. However, many of the woodland species found there also occur around Scapa Flow. The scatter of Aspen, willow scrub, scrambling wild roses and Honeysuckle found on the cliffs around Waulkmill Bay in Orphir, for example, may not look like woodland. However, this has a woodland flora and fauna, from foliage-feeding insects and breeding Willow Warblers to scarce woodland plants such as Hay-scented Buckler-fern.

Underground, strands of fungal tissue form a network that taps into sugars from the roots of trees, providing water and minerals in return. This mutually beneficial arrangement is vital for the survival of trees in these harsh conditions. The relationship goes hidden for most of the year, but wet spells in autumn produce a flush of toadstools of milkcap, brittlegill and bolete fungi, showing something of what lurks amongst the roots and through the thin soils throughout the year.

The wooded stream valley above the kirkyard by The Bu on Hoy holds a very special tree. Here stands a Hazel, one of only three surviving before local conservationists started to propagate more plants from these precious specimens. Nearby, around Quoys and the Whaness Burn, the Downy Birch can be found. Further south on Hoy, another hotspot for native trees can be found where the Pegal Burn meets Scapa Flow – the burn's steep slopes are lined with Aspen, Rowan and willows.

It can just about be argued that Orkney's highest hills also have patches of tree cover of a sort, albeit just an inch or two tall! The Dwarf Willow's home is windswept stony mountain tops, where its tiny twiggy branches run along the ground. It can survive here thanks to its intimate relationship with fungal partners, mirroring the lifestyle of its relatives, the Eared Willow, Grey Willow, Creeping Willow and Tea-leaved Willow which occur much nearer sea-level around Scapa Flow.

Rowan and Aspen on the Hoy coast, with Rysa Little beyond. (Jenny Taylor)

Aspen at Waulkmill Bay, Orphir. (Jenny Taylor)

Aspen near the mouth of the Burn of Sale, The Bring, Hoy. (Jenny Taylor)

Fly Agaric towering above the Dwarf Willow and Heather on the top of Ward Hill, and looking down on Hoy Sound, Graemsay, Stromness and the Bay of Ireland. (Derek Mayes)

Aspen at The Pinnacles, Pegal Bay, Hoy. (Jenny Taylor)

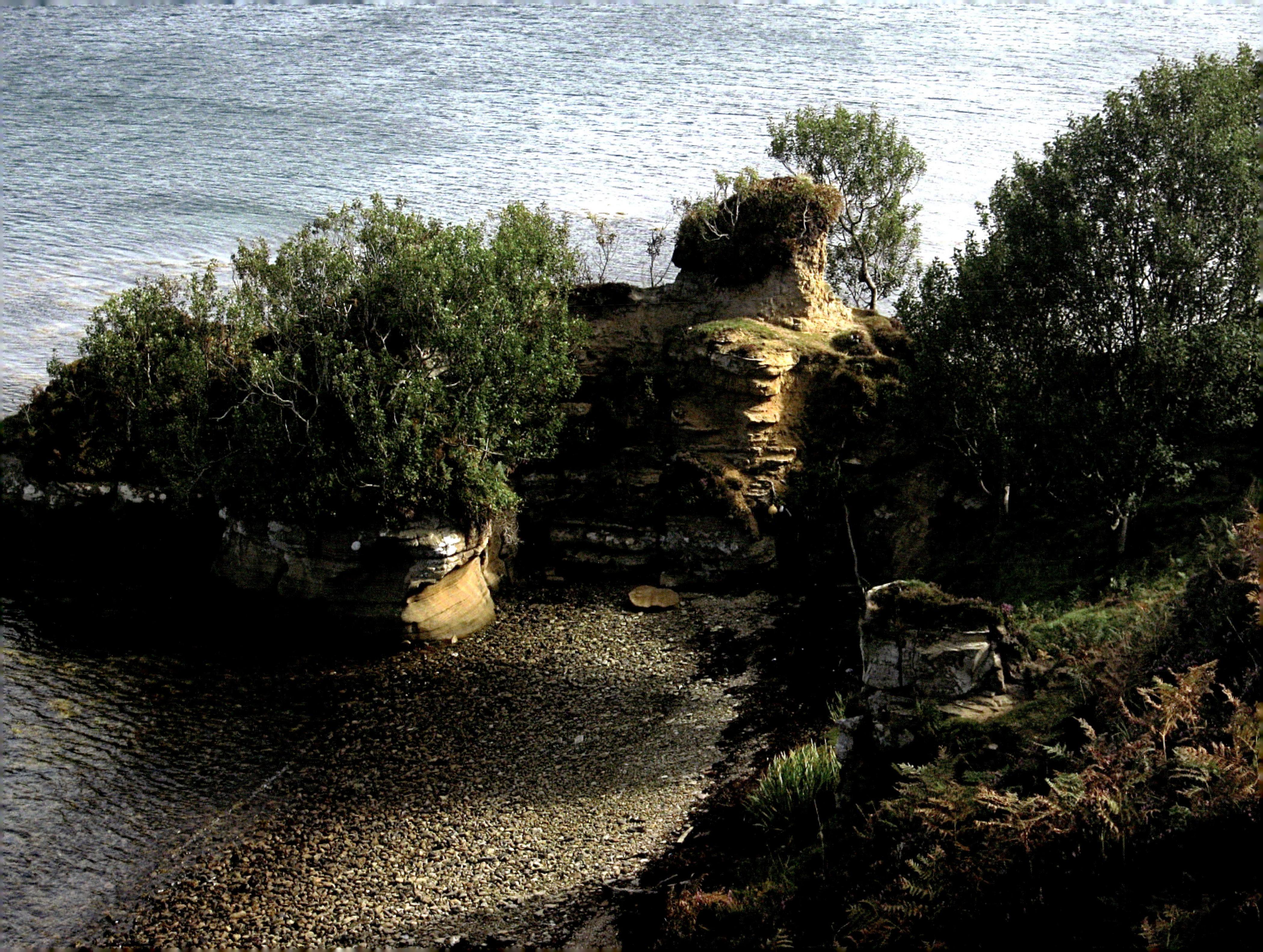

28 Whales and dolphins

A broad range of whales and dolphins can be encountered in Scapa Flow. The most frequent species is the Harbour Porpoise.

Single individuals or small family groups of Porpoise can occur anywhere in the Flow, but Hoxa and Switha Sounds seem to be particular hotspots for them. They are resident in the area all year round, but their small fins are hard to spot unless the sea is very calm. Common Dolphins, Atlantic White-sided Dolphins and Risso's Dolphins are all occasional visitors.

Minke Whales are the most regular of the larger cetaceans. They are filter feeders, having plates of baleen inside their mouths to sift out tiny crustaceans and fish. They are most frequent in the deeper water around Hoxa Sound, but they will also feed in shallower bays.

Killer Whales (also known as Orcas) have become commoner over the years. Most summers bring several sightings. The Orcas can sometimes be seen catching Common Seals.

Pilot Whales, called 'Caaing' Whals' in Orkney, were once herded ashore and killed for their oil-rich blubber. The last whale hunt in Orkney was in 1891. There have been few records in recent years, but this species has a habit of coming into shallow water in large groups, and future Pilot Whale sightings can be expected in Scapa Flow.

Over the years, several groups of up to seven Sperm Whales have been seen in the Flow. In March 1993, a pod of six juvenile male Sperm Whales arrived to spend several weeks in Scapa Flow. When they did not leave, concerns for their survival grew. An attempt to lure them out by playing underwater recordings of females' calls was to no avail. 'Operation Gentle Shepherd' was then put into action, with several small boats driving the whales towards Hoxa Sound. This worked on the second attempt.

Sperm Whales are not the only large whales to have been recorded in the Flow in recent years. In spring 2012, Magnus Spence was out in his boat when he came across a struggling Humpback Whale. Being a scallop diver, he went in to investigate, and found that the whale was tangled in an old creel line. Despite the risk to himself, he managed to cut the whale free, actions which got him much admiration and appreciation.

Porpoise breaching in Switha Sound. (Anne Bignall/SFLPS)

Orcas off Stromness. (Jim Burke)

Female Minke Whale feeding in Echnaloch Bay, Burray; a calf was also present. (Michael Meadows)

Orca at the stern of the mv *Sheila C* off Hoxa Head. (Magnus Spence)

This photo captures an emotional moment when two Common Dolphins joined the mv *Valkyrie*, a Scapa Flow dive boat, on a dive trip in memory of Royal Navy serviceman, Steve Cheshire, after he had died in a diving accident. (Helen Hadley)

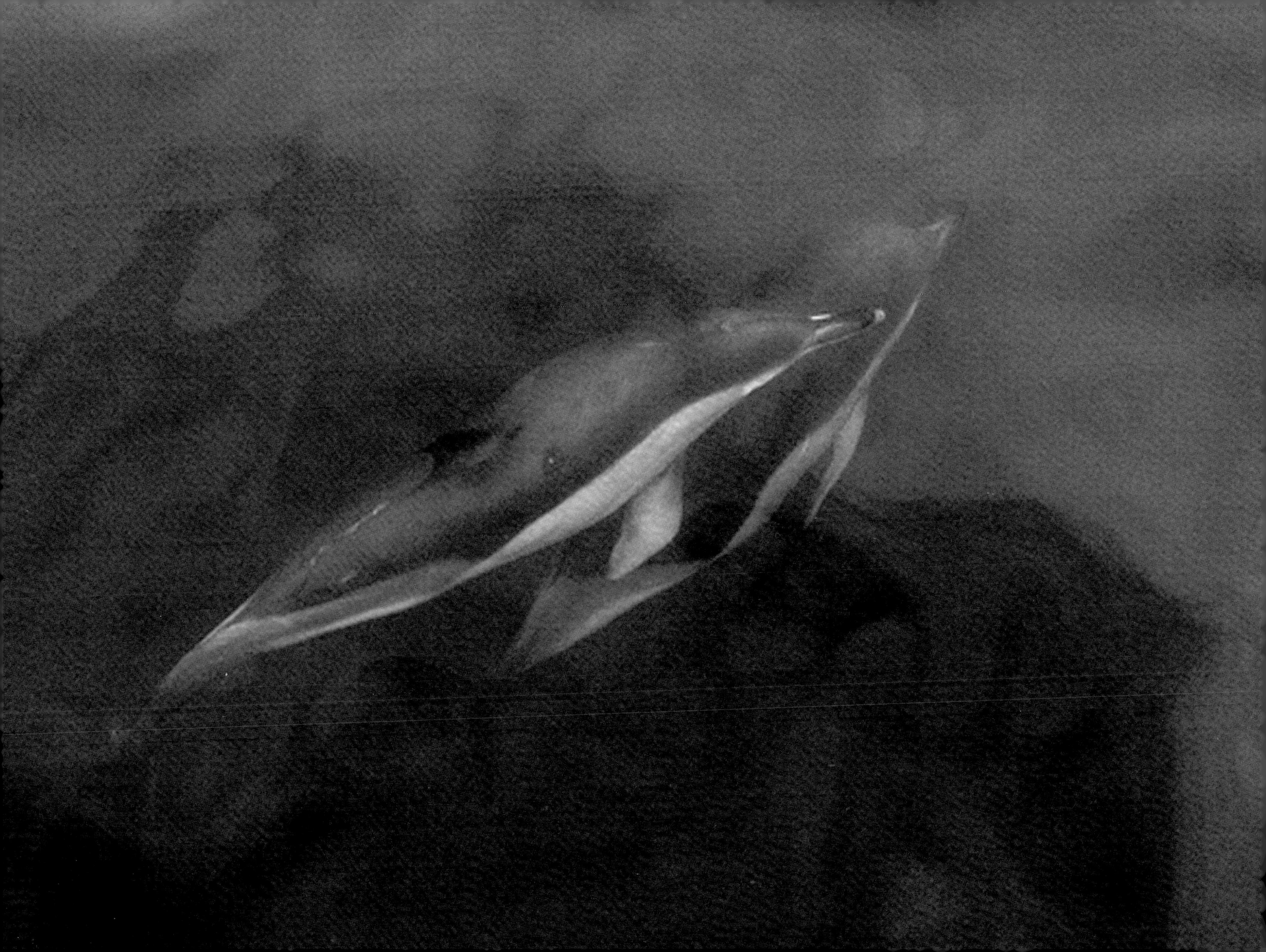

Common Seal relaxing in Bay of Ayre, Holm. (Drew Kennedy)

Common Seals off Holm. (Raymond Besant)

29 Seals

The Common (or Harbour) Seal and the Grey Seal are both to be found around Orkney. Despite the name, the Common Seal is in decline and this species is a lot scarcer than the Grey Seal in Orkney.

Both seal species are known locally as selkies, but Common Seals were also known as 'tang fish' from the Old Norse word 'þang', meaning 'seaweed'. Scapa Flow is an important area for Common Seals in Orkney. An adult male weighs about 85kg and measures 1.5 metres long while an adult female is slightly smaller.

The deadly 'phocine distemper virus' decimated Common Seal numbers in 1988. This disease led to Ross Flett opening Orkney Seal Rescue for the care of sick and injured seals and abandoned pups. It is a Registered Charity based in South Ronaldsay.

The Grey Seal abounds around Orkney, where they were known as 'haaf fish' from the Old Norse 'haf', meaning deep sea. Of the 19,000 Grey Seal pups born in Orkney each year, 1,500 are on remote beaches around Scapa Flow.

They are much larger than the Common Seal; an adult male can weigh 300kg and reach two metres in length. They have more of a 'Roman nose' profile than the Common Seal, which has a smaller and more dog-like head.

Grey Seals give birth in late autumn, particularly November. Grey Seal pups have a white coat for the first three weeks of life. They cannot safely take to the sea until they have been weaned, after about four weeks. In contrast, Common Seals give birth in the months of June and July.

Grey Seal mother and pup. (Anne Bignall/SFLPS)

The pups have already moulted their white coat in the womb, meaning that they can leave the pupping beach and join their mothers in the sea at the first high tide. They are weaned at around six weeks of age.

Tagging of seals has shown that the Grey Seals can travel great distances, as far south as Holland, north to Norway and Faroe and south-west to Ireland. In contrast, Common Seals tend to be more sedentary.

Common Seal on Hunda. (Mark Ferrier)

Inquisitive Grey Seal at Houton. (Penny Martin)

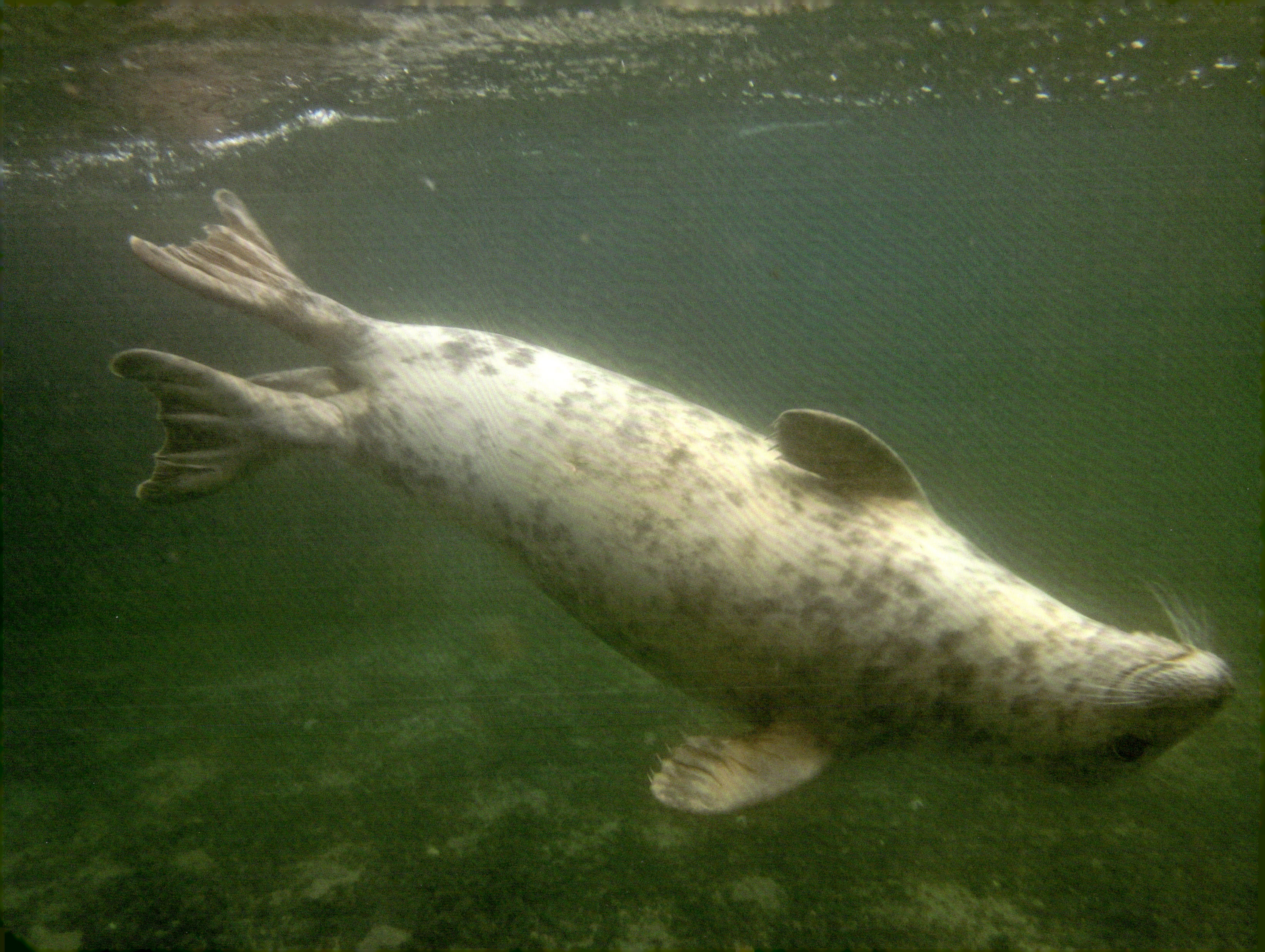

30 Eelgrass

Eelgrass or seagrass – known as 'maalo' in Orkney – is one of the world's very few marine flowering plants. A single species, *Zostera marina*, occurs in Orkney. Eelgrass gets its name from having elongated leaves and forming large underwater meadows, but it is not a true grass.

Eelgrass meadows generally occur below the low tide mark, in sheltered sandy or muddy bays. It requires sunlight to photosynthesise and so exists only in shallow water. Widewall Bay in South Ronaldsay is home to Orkney's largest Eelgrass meadow but smaller stands occur elsewhere around the Flow.

The Eelgrass growing season is from March to September. During this time, plants can grow luxuriantly and beds often become tall and dense – sometimes up to a metre high. In autumn many leaves become detached and get washed ashore, leaving the root system intact to grow another year.

Eelgrass beds support a huge amount of marine life. They provide ideal nurseries for fish such as Pollock and species of wrasse. Two-spotted Gobies move around the bed in small groups. Fifteen-spined Sticklebacks and the Greater Pipefish find safety camouflaged amongst the densely packed blades.

Many species find a home on the Eelgrass itself, including a myriad of microscopic algae and larger animals. Sea squirts are common; colonies of the Star Ascidian and its close relative *Botrylloides leachii* can wrap around sections of a leaf, creating a brightly coloured, patterned sheath. Solitary squirts, like the elegant Gas Mantle Sea Squirt, take an elevated position on the leaves from which to filter their food from the seawater. Molluscs such as Cowries (called Groatie Buckies in Orkney) and Topshells, along with small crustaceans and starfish move over the leaves searching for food.

The root systems of Eelgrass bind the soft sediments, creating habitat for a rich fauna, such as a wide range of worms and molluscs. Amongst these is the Peacock Worm, which quickly retracts its impressive tentacles when it senses an unusual movement in the water column.

In the 1920s and 1930s, a fungal disease decimated the Eelgrass population across the world, although there has been some recovery since. Physical damage caused by dredging for shellfish can have a serious impact. Eelgrass thrives in clear water with low nutrients, so pollution can also take its toll. The great vulnerability of Eelgrass meadows means they have been made a Priority Habitat in the UK Biodiversity Action Plan.

Gas Mantle Sea Squirt in an Eelgrass bed. (Penny Martin)

Greater Pipefish camouflaged amongst the Eelgrass. (Anne Bignall)

Long-spined Sea-scorpion are commonly encountered in the cover of Scapa Flow's Eelgrass beds. (Anne Bignall)

Peacock Worm at Widewall Bay, South Ronaldsay. (Anne Bignall)

Mermaid's Tresses seaweed and Eelgrass catching the sun. (Anne Bignall) ▶

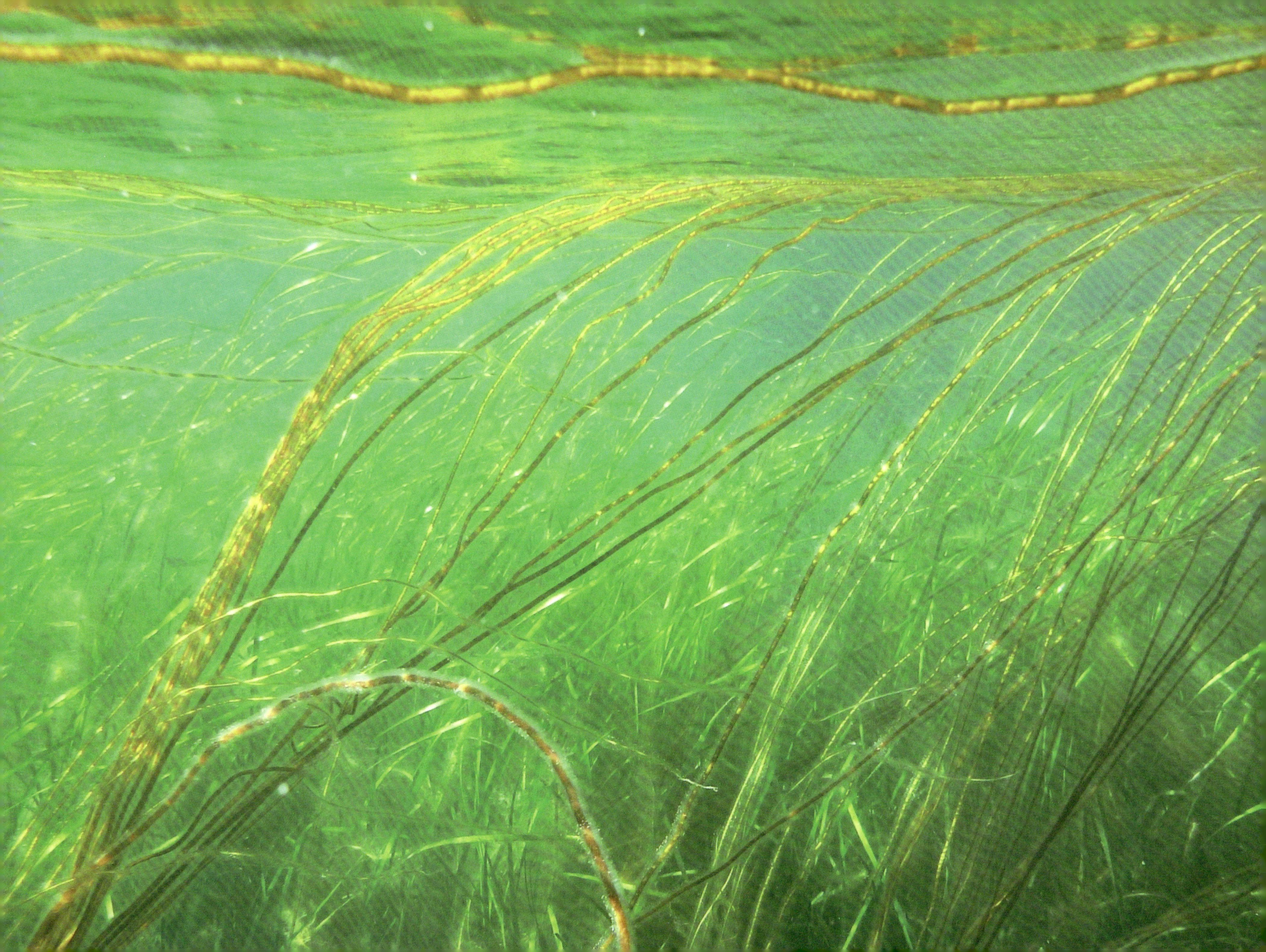

31 Wreck wildlife

No sooner has a shipwreck settled on the bottom of the sea than nature lays claim to it. There are many wrecks on the seabed of Scapa Flow, from mighty warships to the fragile remains of crashed aircraft. Each one creates an artificial reef full of life. Some wrecks are shallow and are colonised by encrusting algae as well as sedentary animals. On deeper wrecks, limited light means animal life dominates, forming a 'faunal turf' over the structure.

Soft corals called Dead Man's Fingers hang down from the superstructure and fittings, while its small but harder relation, the Devonshire Cup Coral, provides a brilliant splash of colour. Many wrecks are home to thousands of Plumose Anemones. When expanded, their numerous tentacles fan out from a robust column that can be up to 30cm high, making an impressive sight.

Sea squirts, which filter plankton from the water that they siphon through their bodies, are common on the wrecks. Some are colonial, like the Star Ascidian, which forms a patterned gelatinous mat on some of the shallower wrecks. Others such as *Ciona testinalis* (sometimes known as Yellow-rimmed Sea Squirt) live singularly. Among the other filter-feeding animals are sponges. Some, like the Elephant's Hide Sponge, form a thick encrustation while other species create branching colonies.

The Common Sea Urchin grazes algae and the faunal turf, making it a frequent sight on wrecks – as well as in most other habitats in the Flow. Common Brittlestars and Feather Stars live on the upper surface of the deeper wrecks, sometimes so densely that they can appear like a singular writhing mass.

Starfish, including the Sunstar and Cushion Star, search slowly but relentlessly for prey. Sea slugs are an equally attractive, if diminutive, group of predators. Shallow dives on the blockships at Churchill Barriers are enlivened by encounters with species such as the Orange-clubbed Sea Slug, which feeds on sea mats (encrusting colonies of bryozoan animals).

The Scapa Flow wrecks are a veritable gourmet's larder, containing European Lobster, Edible Crab and spider crabs, although you might have competition from an elusive Octopus. Conger Eels lurk in crevices and numerous fish dart around the wrecks. The undisputed dandies are the brightly coloured Cuckoo Wrasse. Their mottled orange, blue and green markings make them some of the most beautiful fish in Orkney waters.

Lightbulb Sea Squirts and Red Sea Squirts on the hull of the WWI blockship *Reginald* in Weddel Sound. (Penny Martin)

Devonshire Cup Coral on the SMS *Dresden*. (Anne Bignall)

Long-legged Spider Crab on Dead Man's Fingers. (Helen Hadley)

Plumose Anemones on the wreck of the SMS *Karlsruhe*. (Anne Bignall)

Surprising numbers of fish make the wrecks their home – here a silver shoal swim above a Sunstar feeding on the SMS *Brummer*. (Bob Anderson)

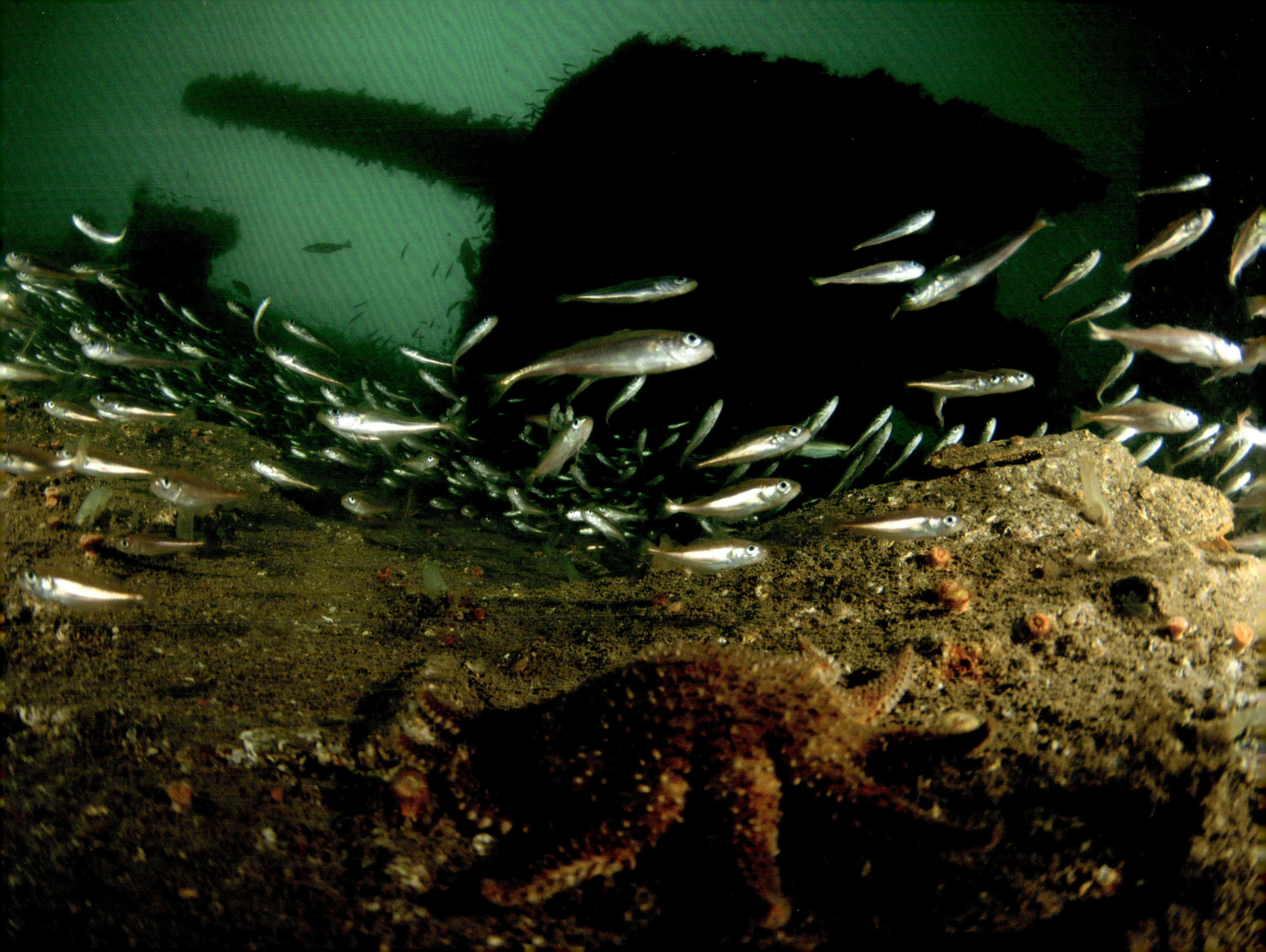

32 Sandy and muddy bottoms

A variety of animals live buried in Scapa Flow's extensive soft sediment, hidden save for any tubes and siphons that protrude above the surface. These include many bivalve shells including the Striped Venus and the delicate Thin Tellin. Other animals like the Sand Mason Worm are only apparent from the small frayed tube made from sand particles and debris, from which they extend white tentacles to trap food.

Scapa Flow supports an important fishery for Great and Queen Scallops. When disturbed, a scallop can try to escape by swimming away from the seabed, propelling itself by a jet of water each time it snaps its shell shut. This has the comic appearance of a set of false teeth, searching hopefully for a lost pensioner.

The Sea Mouse is a bizarre-looking worm densely covered in iridescent hair. It burrows and crawls across the sand and mud, scavenging for dead animals on the Scapa Flow seabed.

Delicate animals live in the softest sediments. The Slender Sea Pen is a feather-like creature which looks more like a plant than an animal which can be seen on the fine muddy sediments in Hoxa Sound, near the wreck of the German WWI submarine *UB-116*.

Flatfish lie camouflaged under a thin layer of sand – their grumpy, sideways faces are often all that is visible. Another predator, the Little Cuttlefish, buries itself in the sand when resting, but darts rapidly in all directions across the surface in search of its prey.

Beds of maerl – also known as Scottish Coral although quite unrelated to true corals – occur off the islands of Graemsay, Cava, Fara and Flotta. Maerl is a collective name for species of 'coralline' algae – red seaweeds that deposit calcium carbonate in their cell walls, giving them a hard, brittle skeleton. The branched nodules of maerl are pink or purple when alive, but turn white when dead. Scallop dredging can easily damage maerl beds, which is ironic as this habitat provides the ideal nursery environment for scallops.

Horse Mussels form important but vulnerable natural reefs. In September 2010, a Horse Mussel bed near the wreck of the SMS *Karlsruhe* was found to be home to a great rarity, the Fan Mussel, which is specially protected. This species can reach nearly 50cm in length, making it the largest shell found in British waters.

A burrowing anemone Cerianthus lloydi. (Penny Martin)

Flounder hiding in the sand alongside Barrier No. 3. (Anne Bignall)

Hermit Crabs are abundant across the seabed. (Anne Bignall)

Fan Mussel near the wreck of the SMS Karlsruhe. (Chris Wood/Seasearch)

A Little Cuttlefish off Stromness. (Dan Wise)

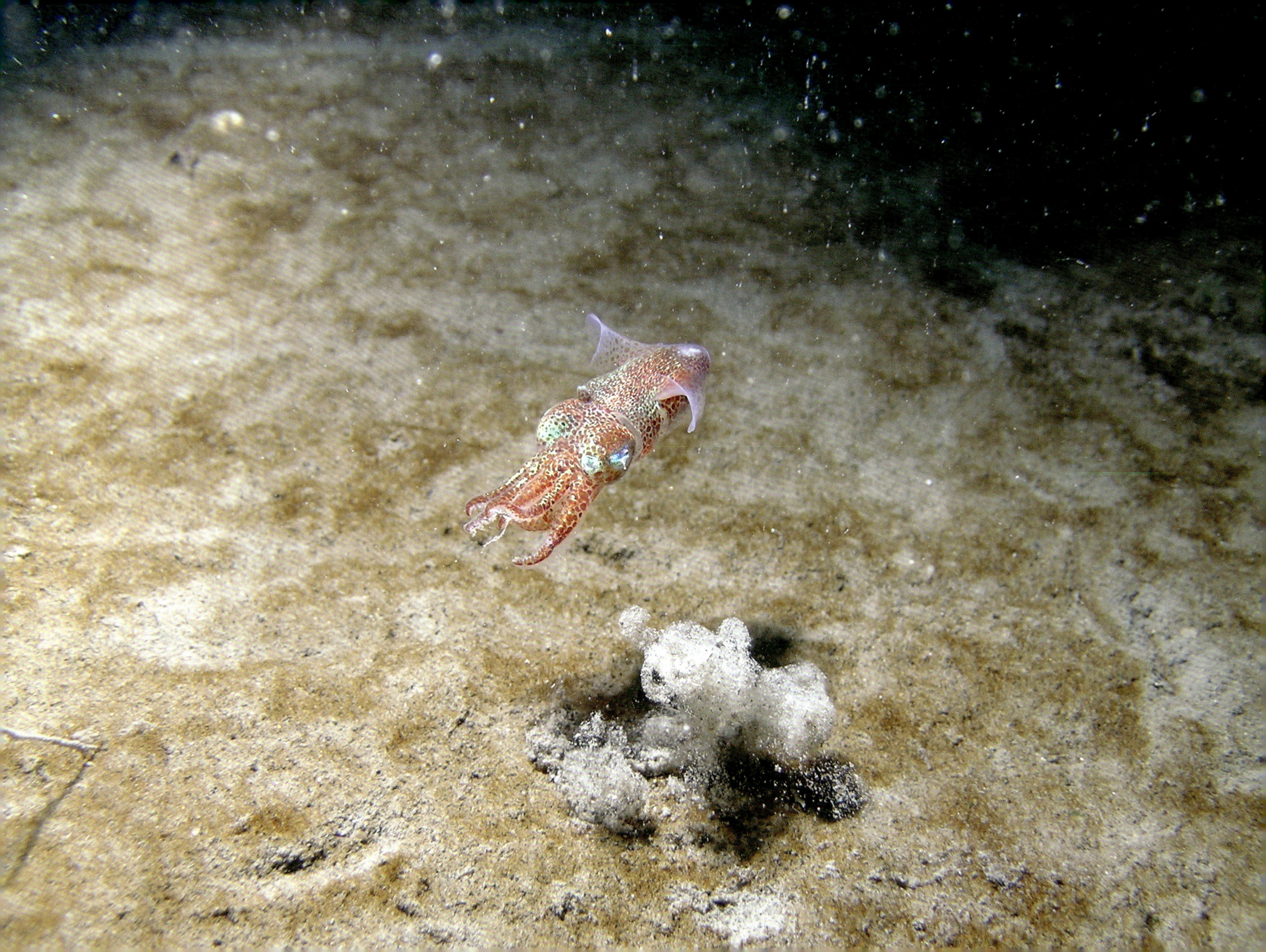

33 Seaweed and kelp forests

Common Urchin amongst seaweeds on the coast of Flotta. (Anne Bignall)

Blue-rayed Limpets on a kelp frond at Barrier No. 2. (Anne Bignall)

Floating Tangle (Oarweed) and Thongweed on the Hoy coast. (Rebecca Marr)

Below low water mark, Scapa Flow's rocky shores support a wonderful range of seaweed-dominated habitat. Searching in the shallows or seeing what is exposed at low tide allows only a glimpse of the impressive array of algal life that lives beneath the surface. When viewed underwater the garden-like qualities of different rocky shores becomes truly apparent.

Areas with an abundance of the green seaweed *Codium fragilis* provide a particularly attractive vista. The sea slug *Elysia viridis* feeds on its erect branching spongy arms. The brown seaweed, Sea Oak, grows in bushy clumps and supports a wide range of life on its fronds including small red seaweeds and invertebrates like hydroids and bryozoans.

Small fish like the Two-spotted Goby shelter in the cover provided by seaweeds. The Long-spined Sea Scorpion lies quietly in wait for unsuspecting prey. Many molluscs graze, scavenge and hunt amongst the seaweeds, including Common Whelks, Edible Whelks and Flat Periwinkles.

Where bedrock is exposed – on shelving slopes below cliffs, on submerged skerries and where currents prevent sediments building up between some of the Scapa Flow islands – the large kelp species dominate. Dense forests of Oarweed and Cuvie can be seen above the surface of the water at low tide whilst Cuvie dominates in deeper water. Dabberlocks and the magnificently architectural Furbelows occur in more exposed locations.

◀ The sea slug *Polycera quadrilineata* eating Sea Mat on a kelp frond at Swanbister Bay, Orphir. (Anne Bignall)

Dabberlocks. (Anne Bignall)

The kelp forests teem with life. They provide shelter and safety for immature Ballan Wrasse, Atlantic Cod and Pollock, and crustaceans, like spider crabs and the Velvet Swimming Crab. The cavities around the holdfast which attaches the kelp to the rock provide an ideal home for many creatures including worms and crustaceans.

The rough stem of Cuvie is often colonised by other algae as well as invertebrates like sponges and sea squirts. The fronds can be covered in other animals including the hydroid *Obelia geniculata* (often known as Kelp Fir) and the bryozoan Sea Mat (*Membranipora membranacea*). Sea Mat is a favourite for grazing sea slugs. A wide array of other molluscs can be found on the kelp; the beautiful Blue-rayed Limpet is present in large numbers in late summer.

Reflections of wracks and kelp in the shallows on a rocky shore at The Lash, Orphir. (Anne Bignall) ▶

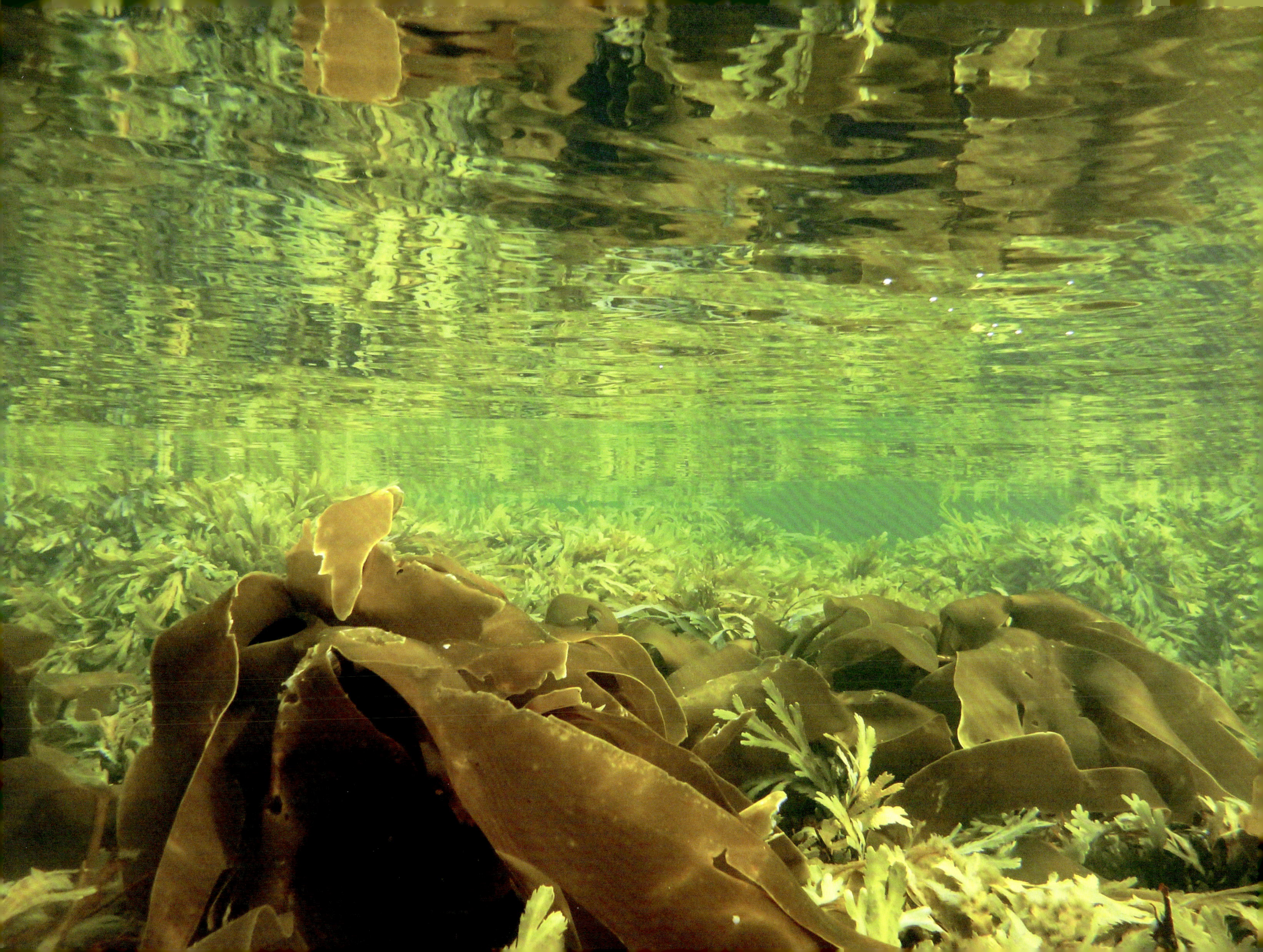

34 Flowers

The land in and around Scapa Flow supports a wide variety of plant life. Across exposed islands and along cliff tops we find maritime heath, made up of small, stunted plants that grow close to the ground and can tolerate the salt spray from the sea. Orkney contains the largest areas of maritime heath that still exist in Britain.

In spring the cliff tops are covered with clumps of Sea Pink (also known as Thrift) with occasional plants of Sea Campion. Spring Squill puts out a carpet of star-shaped blue flowers in its cliff top habitat, while the delicate blooms of Grass of Parnassus twinkle among the short grass, especially where lime-rich water has seeped to the surface.

The salt-loving Sea Plantain grows between crevices in the rocks, while the Sea Arrow-grass also thrives in spray-prone locations, often alongside the Sea Milkwort with its tiny pink flowers. These species are also characteristic of saltmarsh, and are found in patches of this habitat at Brig o' Waithe or Waulkmill Bay for instance, along with other saltmarsh flowers such as Sea Aster.

Down by the shore live more plants that are well adapted for a salty environment. Sea Mayweed grows on sandy or shingle shores and resembles a large daisy. Sea Rocket is found just above the strandline on sandy beaches where it produces a fine display of pinkish coloured flowers. The Oysterplant has fleshy leaves (which are said to taste of oysters) and tiny blue flowers. This Arctic species creeps over the sand and is now colonising the dunes that have built up along the eastern side of Barrier No. 4.

Cliff top vegetation is often heathy in character, or gives way to heaths just inland. These may be a mix of Common Heather (Ling), Bell Heather and Crowberry. Tormentil, a member of the rose family with tiny yellow flowers, adds a splash of colour to heaths.

Damper areas of heathland and bog provide habitat for Common Cotton-grass and other members of the sedge family, along with insectivorous plants such as Butterwort and Sundew. Wet grassland and heathland often has a fine display of the purple buttons of Devil's Bit Scabious in late summer. This herb was used as a cure for scabies, but that infuriated the Devil who bit off part of its root to try to diminish its healing properties.

The hybrid marsh orchid *Dactylorhiza x formosa* on Hoy. (Eric Meek)

Common Cottongrass on West Hill, Flotta. (Rebecca Marr)

Sea Campion on the cliffs of Hoy. (Rebecca Marr)

Spring Squill. (SFLPS)

Thrift framing the view around the northern tip of Hoy and into Hoy Sound beyond. (Derek Mayes)

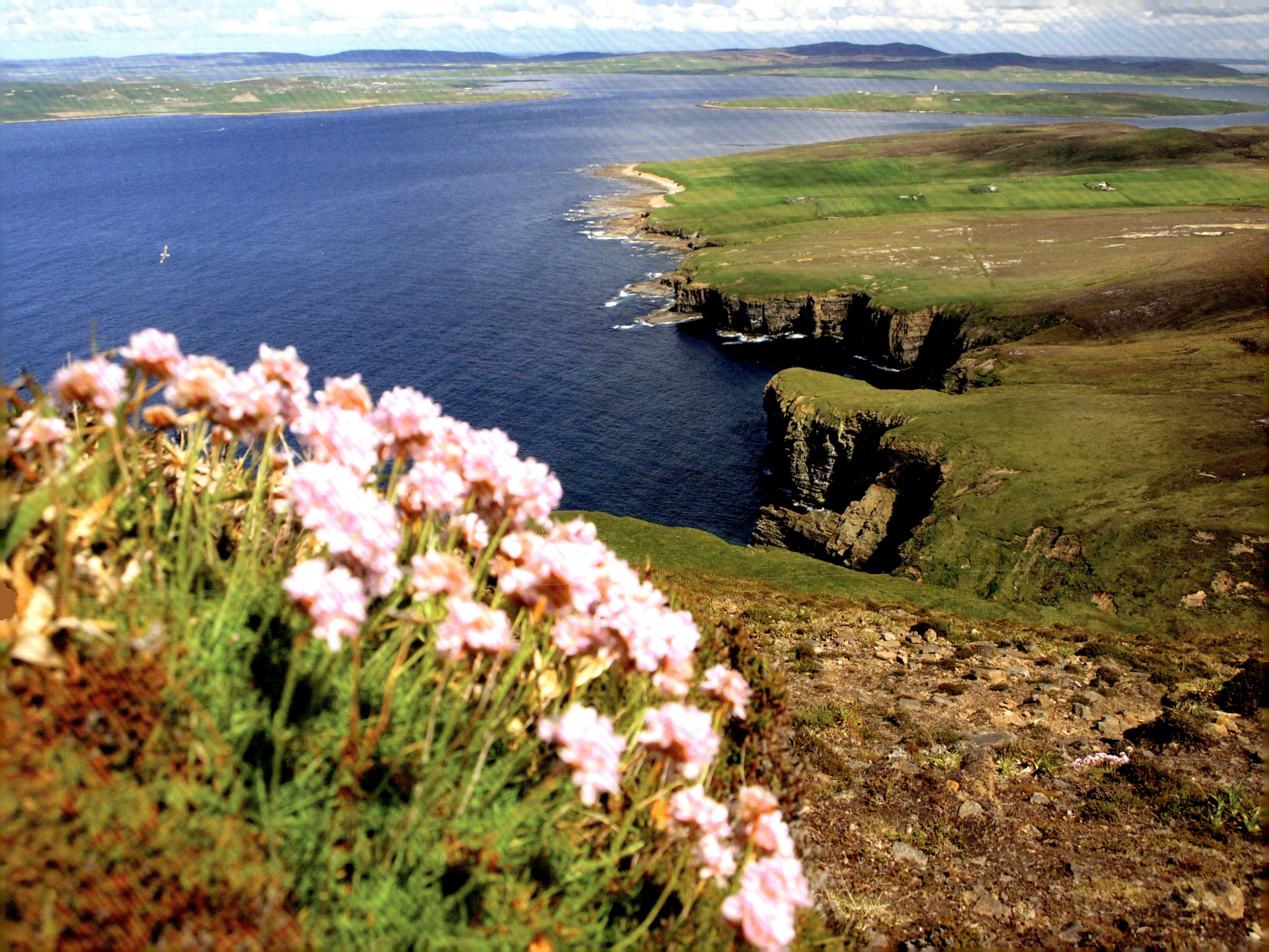

Flat Periwinkle on the coast of Fara – a characteristic species of seaweed-covered rocky shores. (Anne Bignall)

Lyrawa Bay, Hoy. (Raymond Besant)

Lugworm casts in the sand at Lyrawa Bay. (Raymond Besant).

Cockle at Waulkmill Bay. (Raymond Besant)

35 The shore

Twice daily, the tides uncover a great variety of habitat around Scapa Flow, from sandy beaches like Waulkmill Bay and Scapa Bay to long stretches of rocky shores.

At low tide, brown seaweeds are left in soggy heaps strewn across the exposed rocks. On close inspection, Channelled Wrack, Serrated Wrack, Bladder Wrack and Knotted Wrack can all be distinguished, each being suited to slightly different depth zones. Rock pools also offer a chance to see a variety of seaweeds including pink encrusting algae, the red seaweed *Chondus crispus* and green seaweeds like Sea Lettuce.

Among the seaweed the rocks are covered with Acorn Barnacles and the Common Limpet. Clusters of blue Common Mussels can be found at the lowest point of the tide, attached to the rocks and to each other by strong collagenous strands. Dog Whelks and the edible Common Periwinkle (usually known as Whelks) occur in profusion, as does the smaller Flat Periwinkle, which comes in many colours, from green to orange and yellow, either banded, striped or single coloured.

Shore Crabs scuttle around rock pools or hide under seaweed. The Common Hermit Crab is abundant, as it name suggests, making its home in empty shells of various sizes.

Sandy beaches may appear to contain less variety of life than their rocky counterpart, but they are by no means barren. At low tide, the holes and casts of Lugworms cover the sands. This nine inch long worm lives in a U shaped tunnel and filters sand though its body, digesting the micro-organisms and detritus amongst the sand particles.

Many molluscs live in sandy beaches, including the Common Cockle and the Razor Shell. Razor Shells are known as 'spoots' in Orkney because of the spouts of water that shoot into the air when they dive down into their burrows. They are found on the lower shore where they are caught by trapping them against the side of their burrows with a knife and then digging them out by hand.

Many different species of wading birds patrol the shoreline looking for food. Low tide on seaweedy shores, or spots where burns enter the sea, are also the most likely places to come across an Otter in Orkney.

Algae-covered bedrock in the Bay of Ireland, the only part of Scapa Flow in the parish of Stenness. (Premysl Fojtu)

Waulkmill Bay. (Raymond Besant) ▶

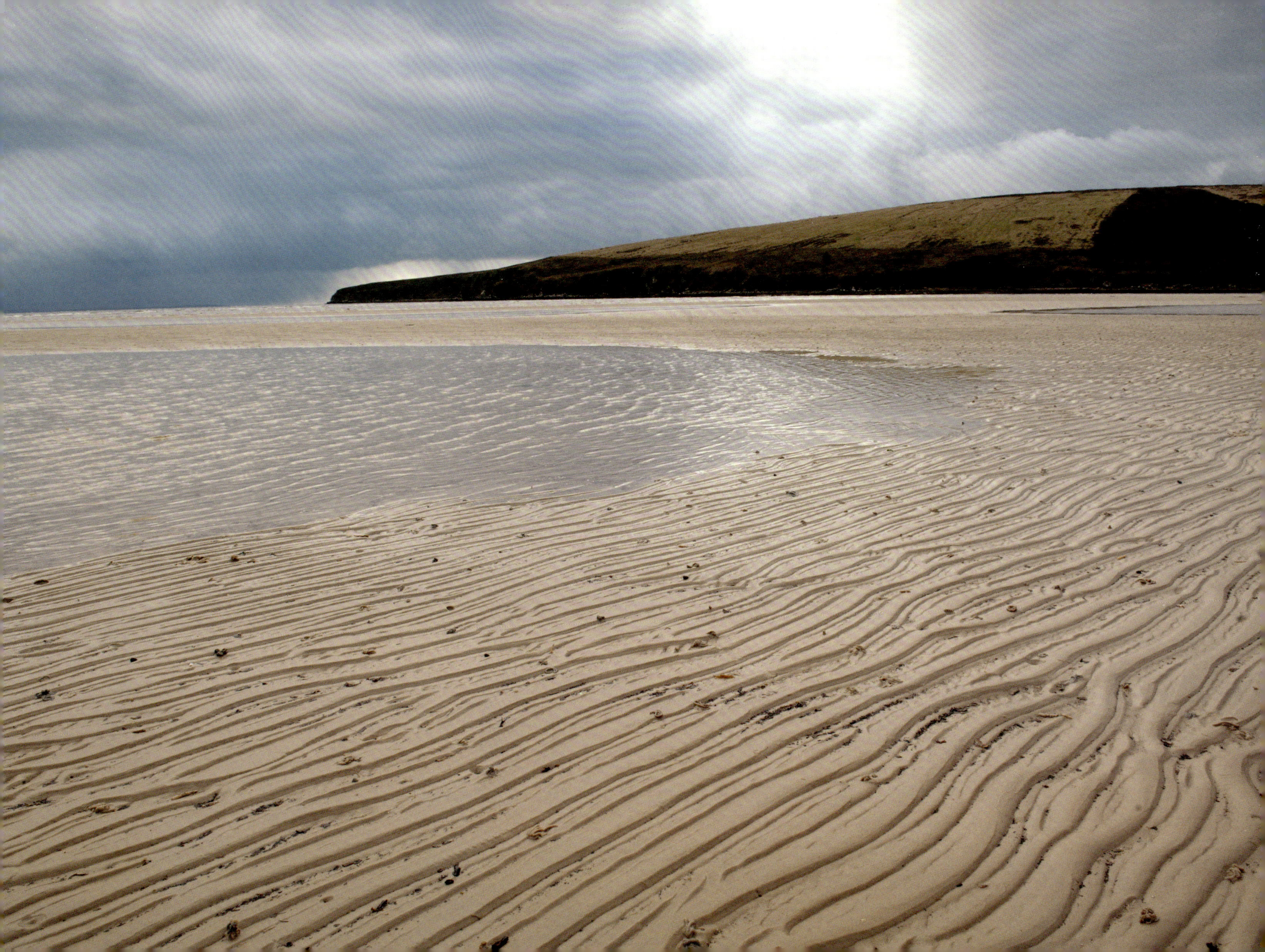

Female Eider in the Bay of Ireland. (Premysl Fojtu)

Oystercatcher nesting along the road to Herston. (Premysl Fojtu)

Bonxie over Stromness. (Gerry Cannon)

36 Birds in summer

Many seabirds come from some distance to feed in Scapa Flow, but some nest around its shores. Everyone's favourite, the Puffin, digs a burrow in which to lay its single egg; both parents take turns in incubation and feed the 'puffling' when it hatches. The uninhabited island of Switha is a popular nesting ground. A few of these characterful birds can also be seen on the cliffs at Hoxa Head and Stanger Head, on either side of Hoxa Sound.

Colonies of Arctic Terns are widespread, but this bird has declined greatly as sandeels have become rarer, no longer providing a reliable source of food for their chicks. Its close relative the Common Tern is poorly-named as far as Orkney is concerned, as it is much rarer here, but the old wooden wartime North Pier at Lyness has a colony of up to 100 breeding pairs.

The availability of eggs and chicks attracts predators such as the Great Skua every summer. These birds, called 'Bonxies' in Orkney, are highly aggressive towards anyone who gets too near to their nests. The Bonxie is a common sight during the summer months – the Scottish islands are its global stronghold. Its vicious predatory habits have given it a bad name amongst many local people. However, the Orkney naturalist Tim Dean has noted that the world has more Polar Bears than it has Bonxies, pointing out Orkney's international responsibility for this species.

These days, one of the most common seabirds in Orkney is the Fulmar, so it is hard to believe that they only colonised Orkney in 1900. With the advent of the steam engine, fishing boats could travel further north, reaching the breeding grounds of the Fulmar in Faroe and Iceland.

White-billed Diver in Water Sound in 2008. Orkney is renowned as a magnet for vagrant birds. Many birdwatchers enjoyed this rare visitor which summered between Burray Village and St Margaret's Hope. (Morris Rendall)

Fulmars started to follow the fishing boats south for the free meal of fish gutting waste and rejected fish.

The Red-throated Diver breeds on the hilltops in Hoy, using small lochans in peat bogs to raise its chicks, but commuting to Scapa Flow's bays to catch fish. It is called the 'Rain Goose' in Orkney as it is supposed to be able to predict the weather; if it flies towards land, or gives short cries, then the weather will be fine but if it flies towards the sea, or gives a long call, it will rain.

Tystie (Black Guillemot) at Lyness, Hoy. Many pairs of this auk find nest sites on the old piers here. (Raymond Besant)

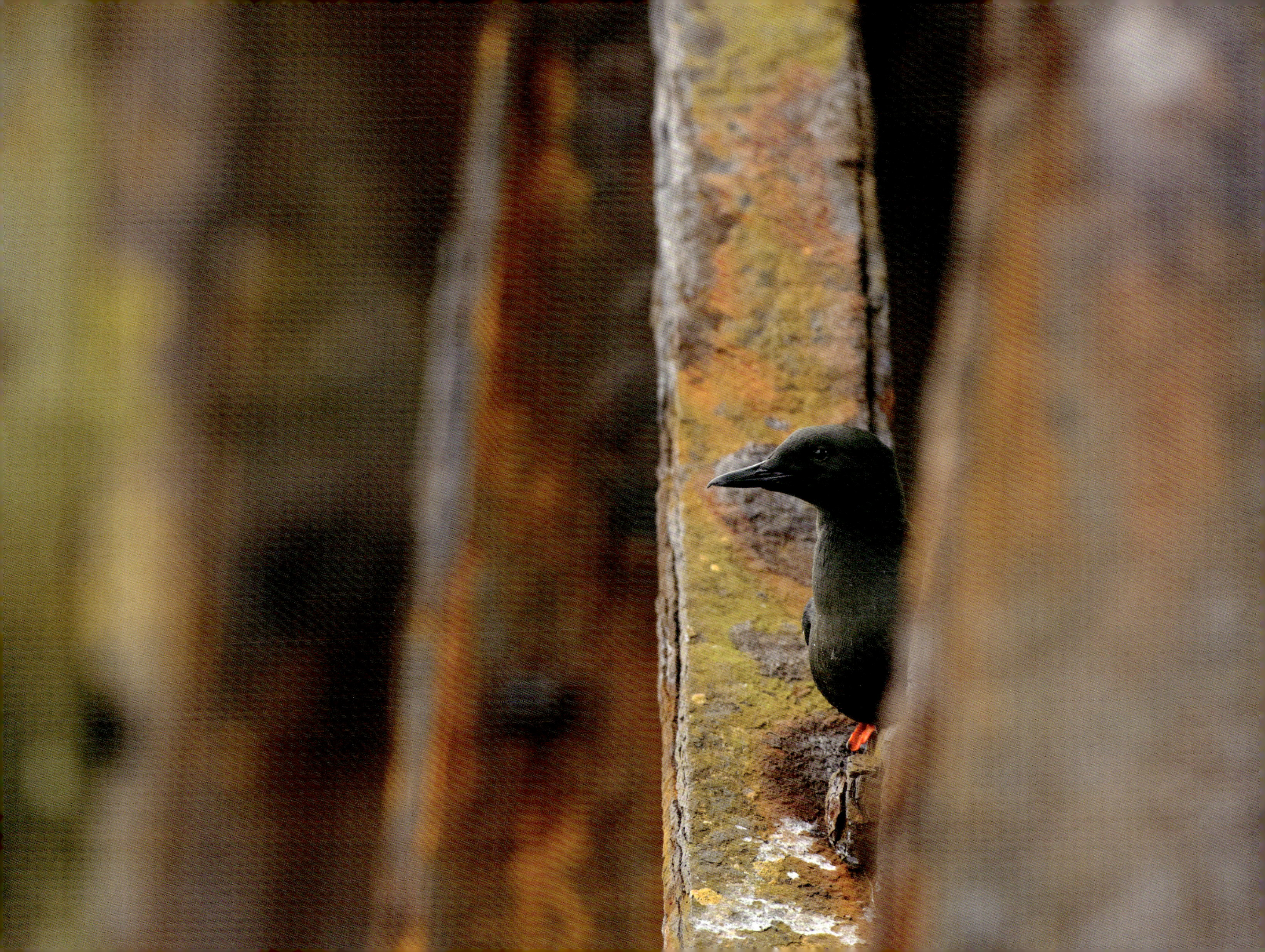

Great Northern Diver in Scapa Flow. (Morris Rendall)

Little Auk just off Scapa Pier. (Ian Cunningham)

Small numbers of Red-breasted Merganser can be seen all round the Scapa Flow coast. (Ian Cunningham)

37 Birds in winter

Winter sees many of the breeding birds leaving Orkney, but others arrive from more northern climes. On the shoreline, resident waders such as the Curlew, Oystercatcher, Redshank and Ringed Plover are joined in their search for food by Purple Sandpiper, Sanderling, Turnstone and Bar-tailed Godwit.

On the fields, Orkney's fast increasing numbers of breeding Greylag Geese are joined by tens of thousands more from Iceland. It seems hard to believe that until recently these geese were quite rare in Orkney, just passing briefly on migration. Now more than half of Britain's wintering population are to be found here.

The delicate and beautiful Barnacle Geese have settled into Switha and South Walls since the 1960s. These globally rare birds were eating so much in this restricted area that a Goose Management Scheme was set up which paid farmers to provide feeding areas and now over 1,500 can be found each winter.

Scapa Flow's resident Tysties (Black Guillemots), Eider Duck and Red-breasted Merganser are joined by numbers of Long-tailed Ducks, with the waters around Flotta and Hunda being particularly good for these striking waterfowl. Around most parts of Britain, Little Auks are only seen when storms drive birds to shore from the open ocean, however the centre of Scapa Flow seems to be a regular haunt for a few, with birds sometimes seen from shore at Scapa, in Bay of Sandoyne in Holm and around the Barriers.

◀ Slavonian Grebes occur in considerable numbers, especially in the eastern part of the Flow. (Ian Cunningham)

Skarfies (Shags) on Lamb Holm against the low sun of a January afternoon. (Raymond Besant)

Great Northern Divers return from their nesting grounds in Iceland, Greenland and Canada, with Scapa Flow being the most important wintering site for them in the British Isles. Black-throated Divers are much scarcer in Orkney, but a tight group of 15 or 20 is usually to be found somewhere in Scapa Flow each winter, either in the coastal waters on the Flow's eastern fringe, or around Fara.

Scapa Flow is also nationally important for the Slavonian Grebe, with well over 100 birds being present at times. They leave in spring to breed in Iceland, Scandinavia and Russia. Small numbers now breed on lochs in the Scottish Highlands; perhaps we can expect some to start to stay and breed in Orkney, given what a wonderful range of freshwater habitat that these islands provide.

Adult Tystie (Black Guillemot) in winter plumage at Lyness, Hoy. (Orkney Photographic) ▶

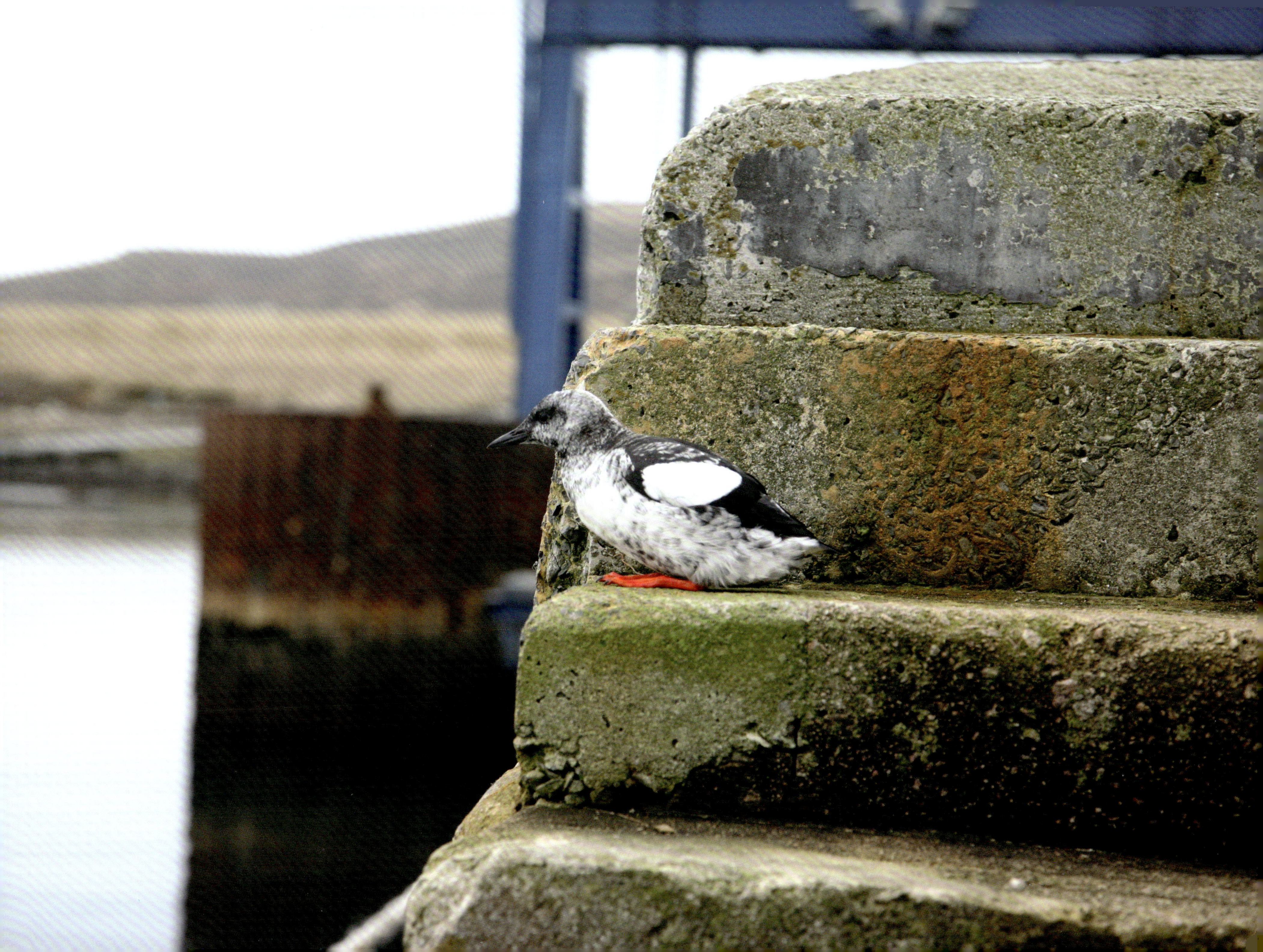

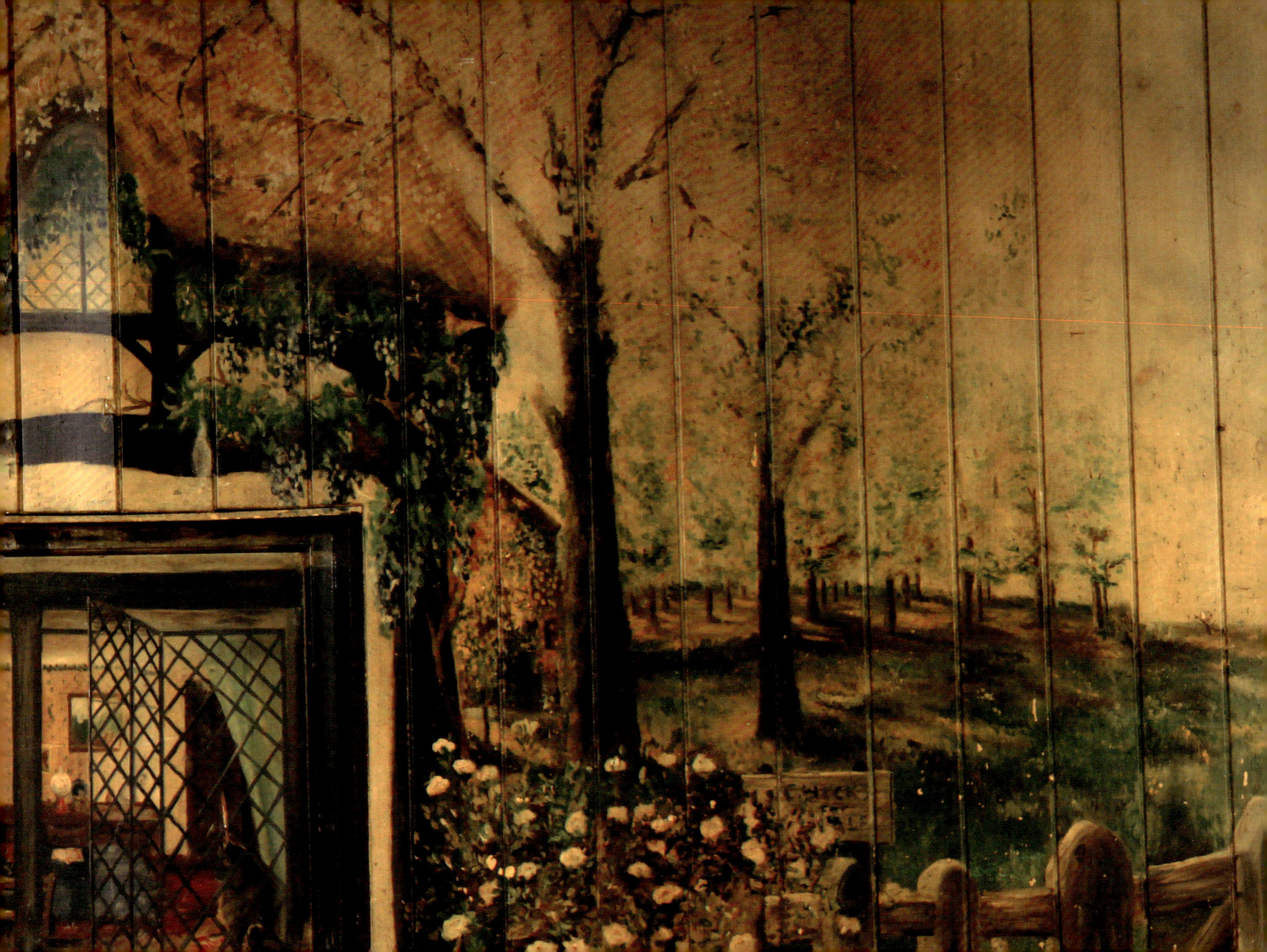

SFLPS projects

Mural at Ness Battery. (SFLPS)

Ness Battery

Restoration work removed a 1970s suspended ceiling, exposing a painted proscenium with the Battery's motto and the emblem of the Royal Artillery. (Photo: Frances Flett Hollinrake)

The mural, painted by AR Woods, has had careful conservation treatment throughout by Scottish Wall Painting Conservators. There was time for yellowed varnish to be painstakingly removed from one area of the mural, showing the brightness of the original colours. (Photo: Andrew Hollinrake)

Project Officer Cathy Fisher stands by the mural in 2010, before restoration took place. (Photo: The Orcadian)

The two 6-inch gun emplacements were in a perilous state when restoration started in 2011, as the 1940s steel frame supporting the emplacement's suspended roof had almost rusted through. A discreet new steel frame is now in place, with the original steelwork now no longer having to provide a structural function. (Photo: Andrew Hollinrake)

(Photo: Andrew Hollinrake)

Before any restoration could start, the whole site needed to be carefully recorded by an archaeological buildings survey, as befitted the site's Scheduled Ancient Monument status. (Photo: Orkney Research Centre for Archaeology)

Ness Battery
OFFICIAL SOUVENIR GUIDE

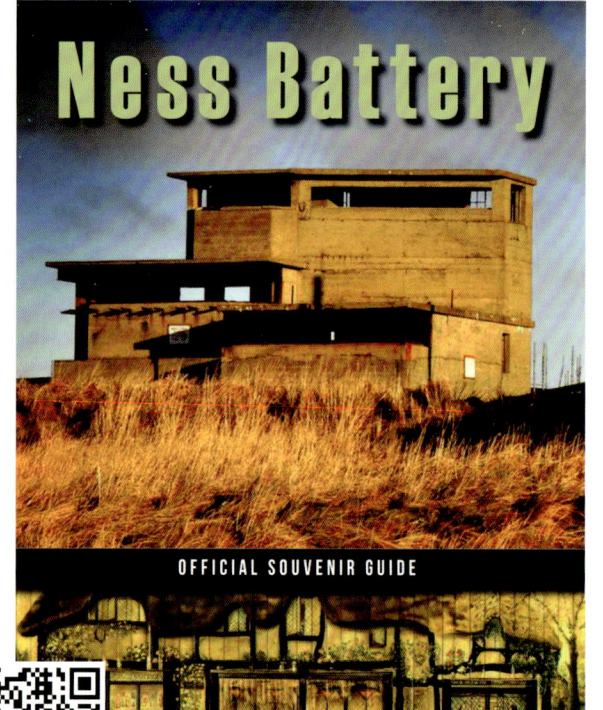

A Ness Battery Souvenir Guide was produced in 2013. It is available from all good booksellers, or for sale via the Ness Battery website. To book a tour, visit www.nessbattery.co.uk, email info@nessbattery.co.uk or call 07759 857298). (Artwork: Iain Ashman)

The tower is one of the most impressive features of the site. It is thought to be unique in its design, which results from the combination of so many functions in one structure – Royal Navy Signal Station, Fire Command for Hoy Sound, Battery Observation Post and Searchlight Direction. (Photo: SFLPS)

The wooden huts – shown here in their freshly restored state in 2012 – are unique, being the only accommodation huts that survive at any coast battery in Britain. The Officers' Mess is in the foreground, the two Other Ranks huts are back left, and the famous Mess Hall and cookhouse are back right. (Photo: Andrew Hollinrake)

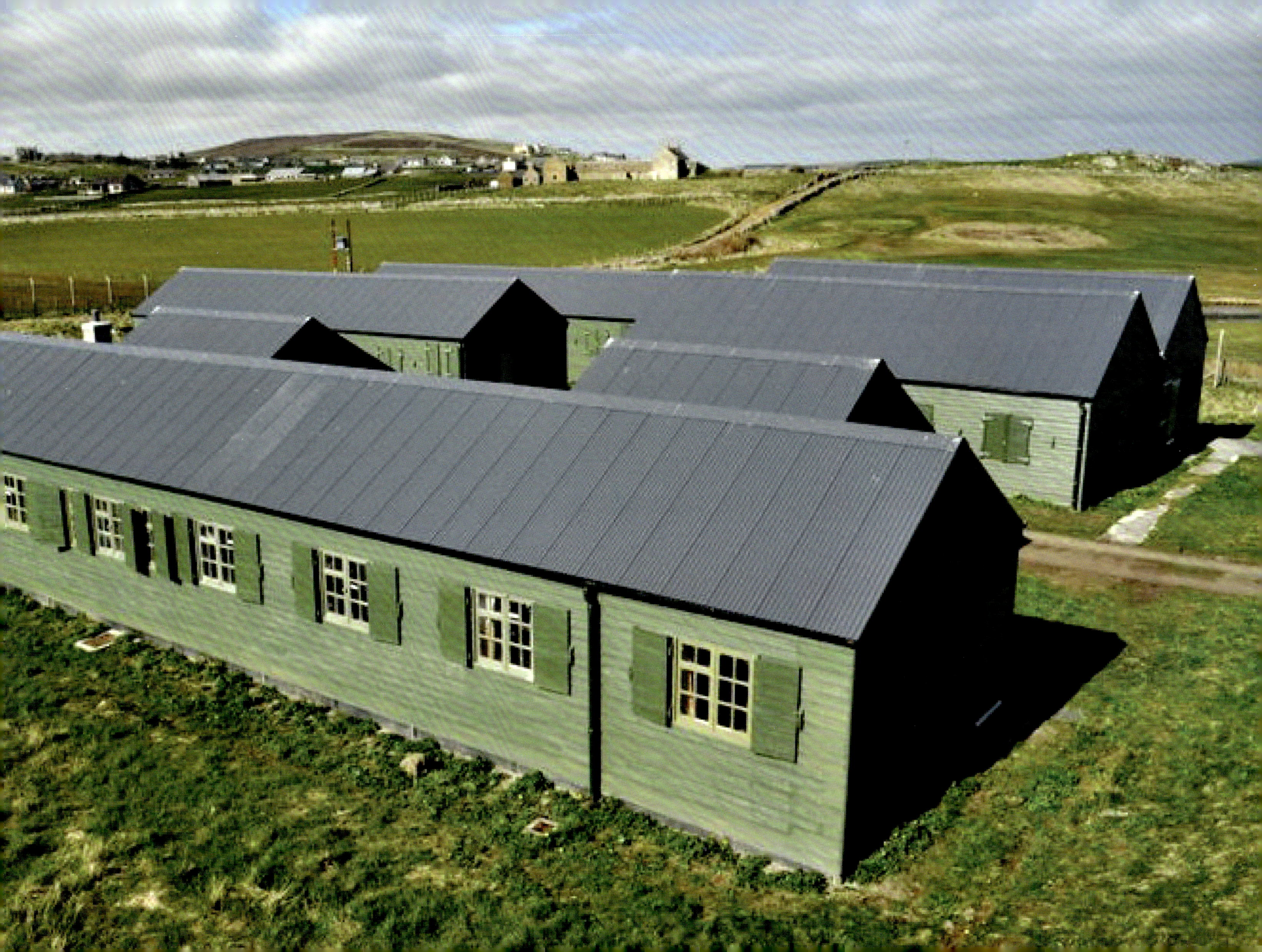

Building the Barriers, remembering and recording, and wildlife beneath the waves

This model showing Barrier No. 3 in three stages towards its completion in World War II, is a striking and informative part of the Building of the Barriers exhibition. (Photo: SFLPS)

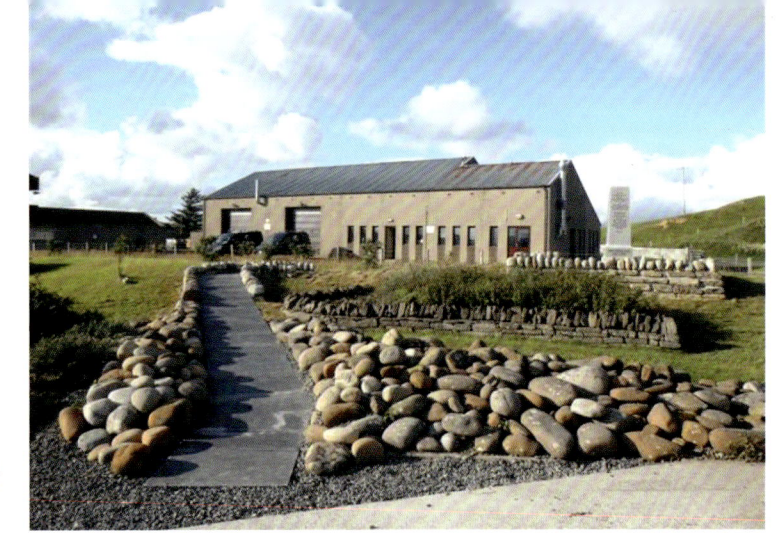

Work to the *Royal Oak* Memorial Garden included construction of an access-for-all pathway, bordered decoratively with beach cobbles, up to the *Royal Oak* memorial. (Photo: SFLPS)

The exhibition details the historic context, engineering achievements and the social and environmental consequences of the Building of the Barriers. (Photo: SFLPS)

The man in the blue coat is Frank Mitchell, who built the model of the Italian Chapel which he has now donated to form part of the exhibition. Also, note the floor map – this has been a surprisingly popular feature! (Photo: SFLPS)

The Building of the Barriers exhibition is housed in the Orkney Fossil & Heritage Centre, in Burray, adding considerably to this fascinating museum. (Photo: SFLPS)

The Scapa Flow Marine Habitats exhibition has also been located at the *Royal Oak* Memorial Garden, highlighting the diversity of wildlife found in Scapa Flow. This series of interpretative panels also promotes the Pick Up 3 Pieces campaign against marine litter developed by Glaitness Primary School. (Photo: SFLPS)

Orkney Research Centre for Archaeology provided a very successful training course in the study and recording of wartime defence archaeology. This photo captures the recording of the Emergency Engine Room close to where the searchlights of Ness Battery were located. (Photo: ORCA)

Looking out into Scapa Flow from the *Royal Oak* Memorial Garden at Scapa. The interpretation panel in the foreground was part of a programme of improvements at this poignant location. (Photo: SFLPS)

Welcome to the Royal Oak Memorial Garden

Batteries, wrecks, Lyness and a lonely grave

Betty Corrigall's grave stands on the lonely hillside near Scad Head. SFLPS has replaced the interpretation which tells the sad story of this young unmarried mother who took her own life and was then buried in a grave (unmarked at the time) on the Parish boundary running across the middle of the island of Hoy. (Photo: SFLPS)

The opening of the Flotta Trail took place in glorious sunshine, with Richard Shearer declaring the trail open by cutting the ribbon with his grandfather's Royal Marine Artillery sword. A highlight of the day was Richard, dressed in his grandfather's Second Lieutenant uniform, showing attendees around the site of the Neb Battery where his grandfather served in World War I. (Photo: SFLPS)

Simple stone markers point out the route across the moorland from the site of a WWII anti-aircraft battery on Lyrawa Hill, Hoy, to the tramline down to the Scad Head Battery. (Photo: SFLPS)

Buchanan Battery is a well-preserved WWII twin 6-pounder battery on Flotta, which is now interpreted from the Flotta Trail. (Photo: SFLPS)

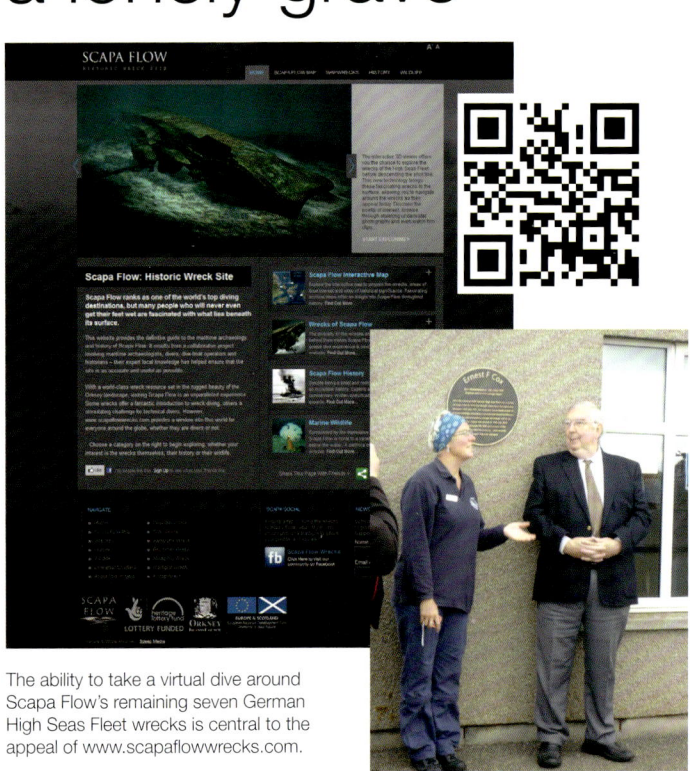

The ability to take a virtual dive around Scapa Flow's remaining seven German High Seas Fleet wrecks is central to the appeal of www.scapaflowwrecks.com.

SFLPS organised a plaque at Lyness to remember the inter-war salvage work on the scuttled German High Seas Fleet. The photo shows Jude Callister, Custodian of the Scapa Flow Visitor Centre & Museum, with Ernest Cox's grandson, Jon Moore, at the unveiling of this plaque to Ernest Cox. (Photo: SFLPS)

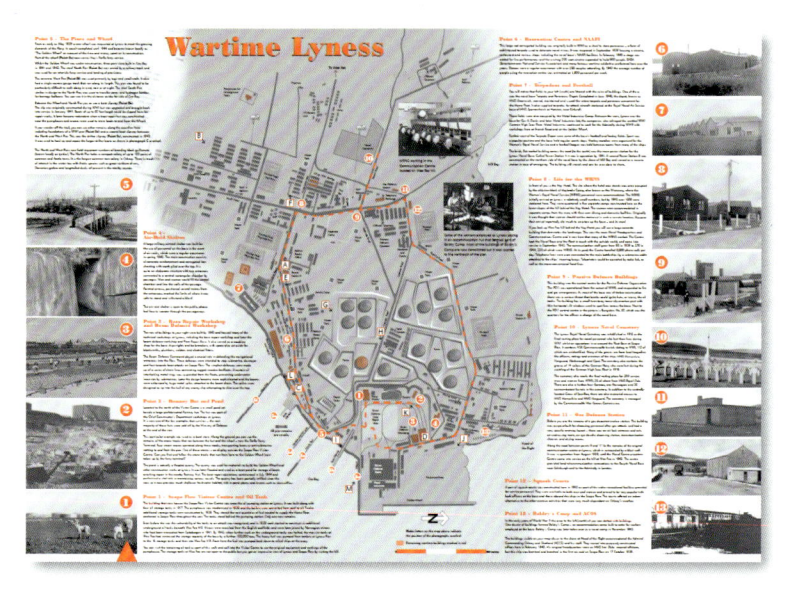

The Lyness Wartime Trail leaflet demonstrates the impressive scale of the WWII naval base at Lyness, adding much to the superb facility already offered by the Scapa Flow Visitor Centre & Museum in the former pumphouse there. (Artwork: Iain Ashman)

Scad Head on Hoy is a remote spot which housed a twin 6-pounder battery to protect the boom defences across Bring Deeps, at the western end of Scapa Flow. SFLPS has marked a walk to encourage people to visit this beautiful and fascinating location – the section of path in the photograph runs down the tramline which connected the battery with the road above. (Photo: SFLPS)

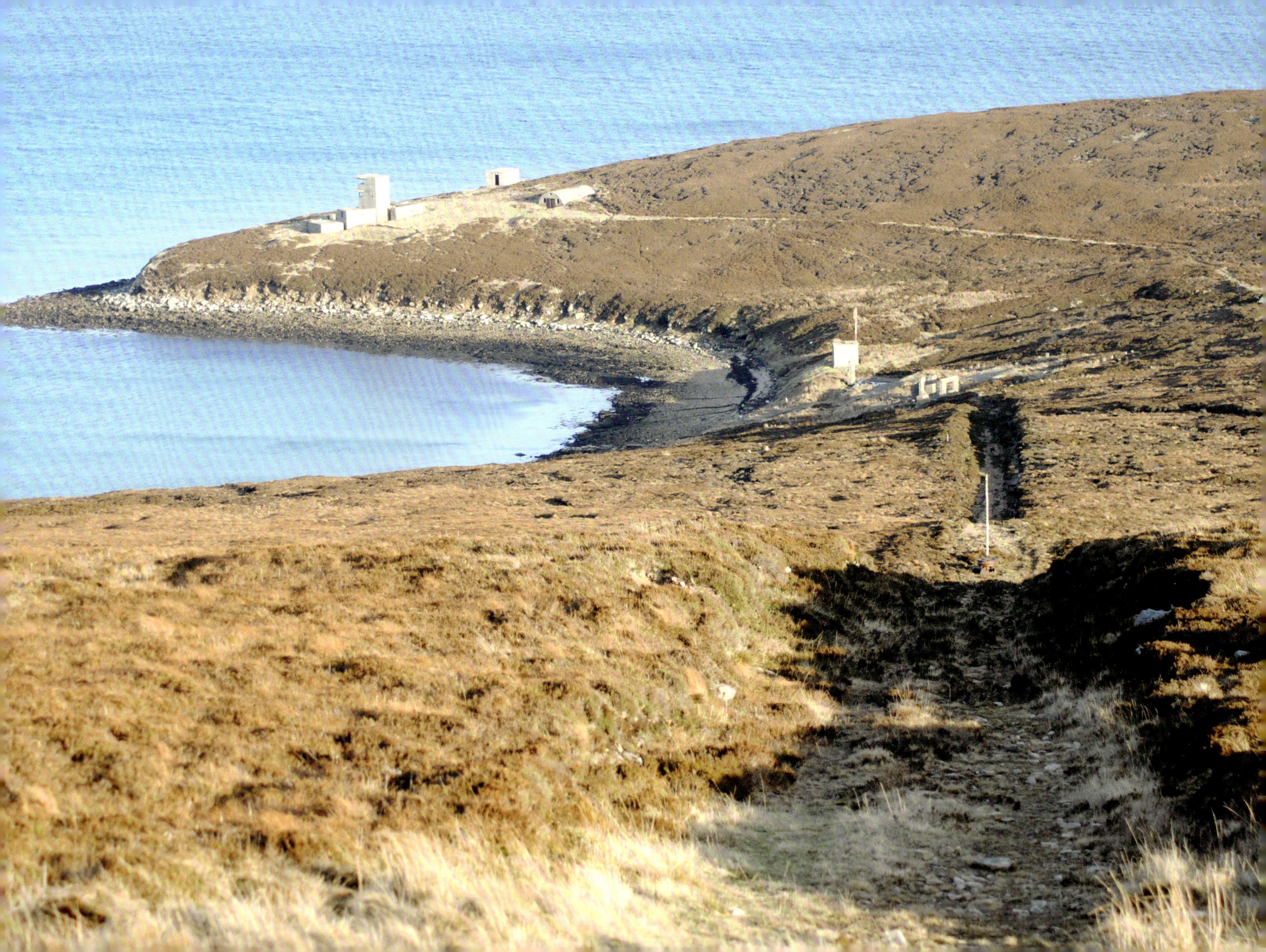

Saga story bench, Osmundwall

Tom Muir, Anne Bignall, artist, and Colin Watson, mason, after the bench was safely erected at Osmundwall, South Walls. (Photo: Andrew Hollinrake)

Colin directs the erection of the bench. (Photo: SFLPS)

Anne Bignall and Colin Watson in conference over his interpretation of her illustration of the *Orkneyinga Saga* story. (Photo: SFLPS)

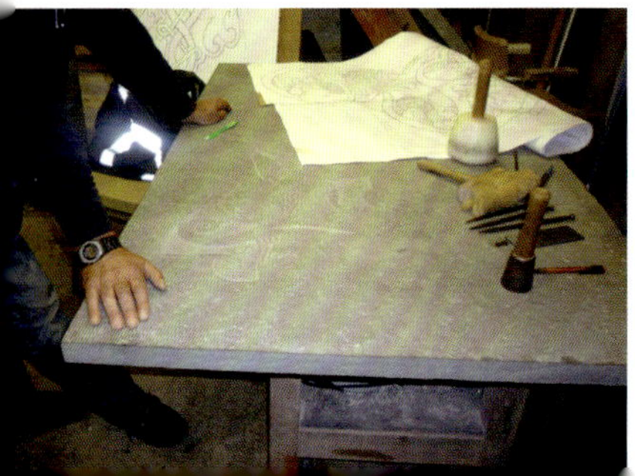

Colin reviews progress of the carving against Anne Bignall's drawings. (Photo: SFLPS)

Tom Muir, author of two books on the *Orkneyinga Saga*, provided interpretation of the *Saga* story, with the creative partnership recorded in a runic inscription on the back of the bench, which translates as "Tom Muir told the story, Anne Bignall did the drawing and Colin Watson set it in stone". The knotwork dragons' heads were inspired by bed-ends from the Oseberg Ship Burial. (Photo: SFLPS)

The bench in situ in the winter afternoon sun. The bench looks out on Kirk Sound, where Earl Sigurd the Stout was forcibly converted to Christianity by Olaf Trygvesson in the year 995 AD. The bench also stands close to the memorial to the tragic loss of the crew of Longhope lifeboat *T.G.B.* in 1969. (Photo: SFLPS)

St Magnus Cathedral mason, Colin Watson, spent many hours to create this bench, which tells the *Orkneyinga Saga* story of the Conversion of Sigurd the Stout. (Photo: SFLPS)

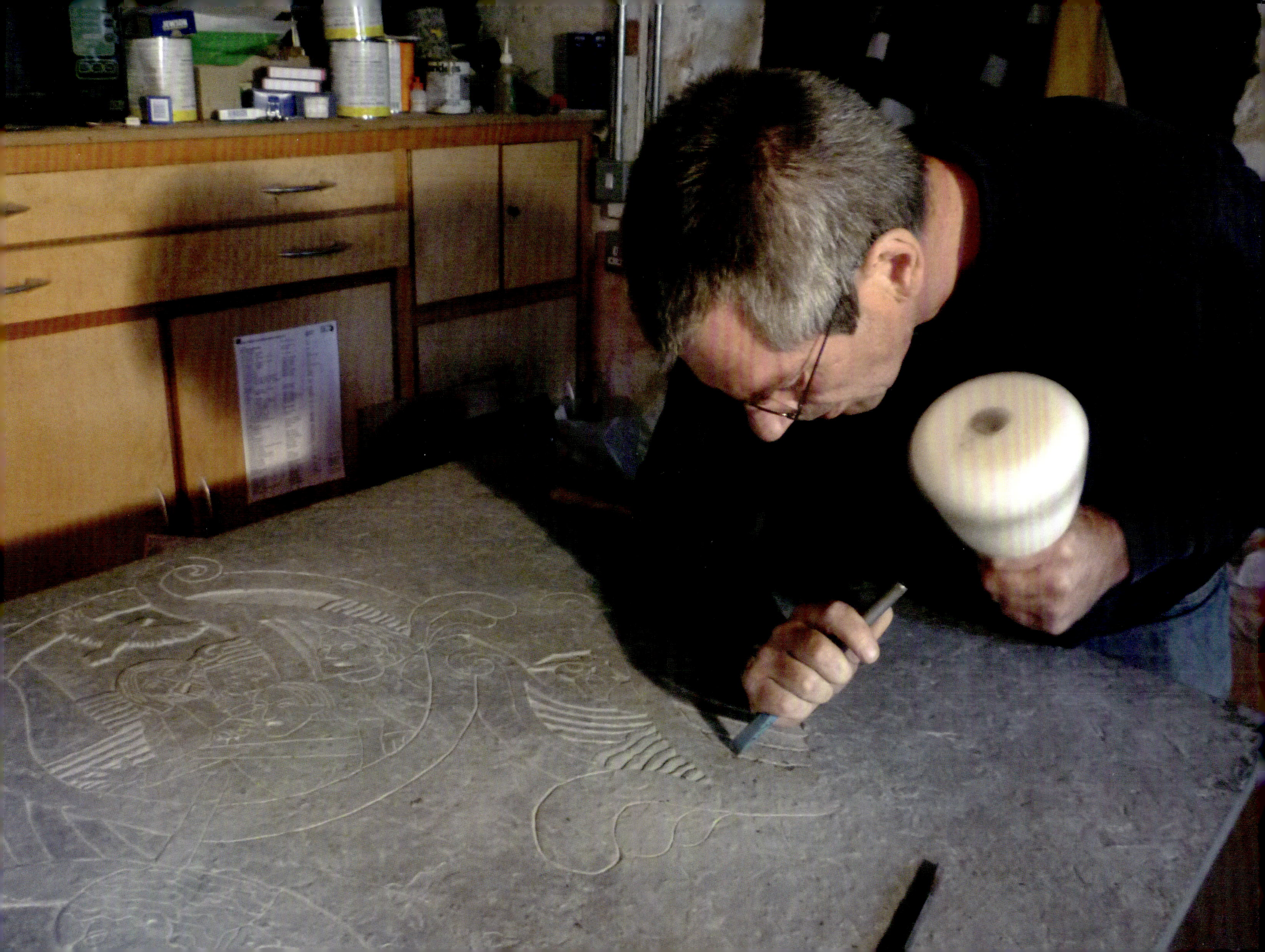

History and archaeology

Caroline Wickham-Jones and her collaborators in the Rising Tide Project expressing satisfaction at the new hunter-gatherer exhibition at Tomb of the Eagles. (Photo: Rising Tide Project)

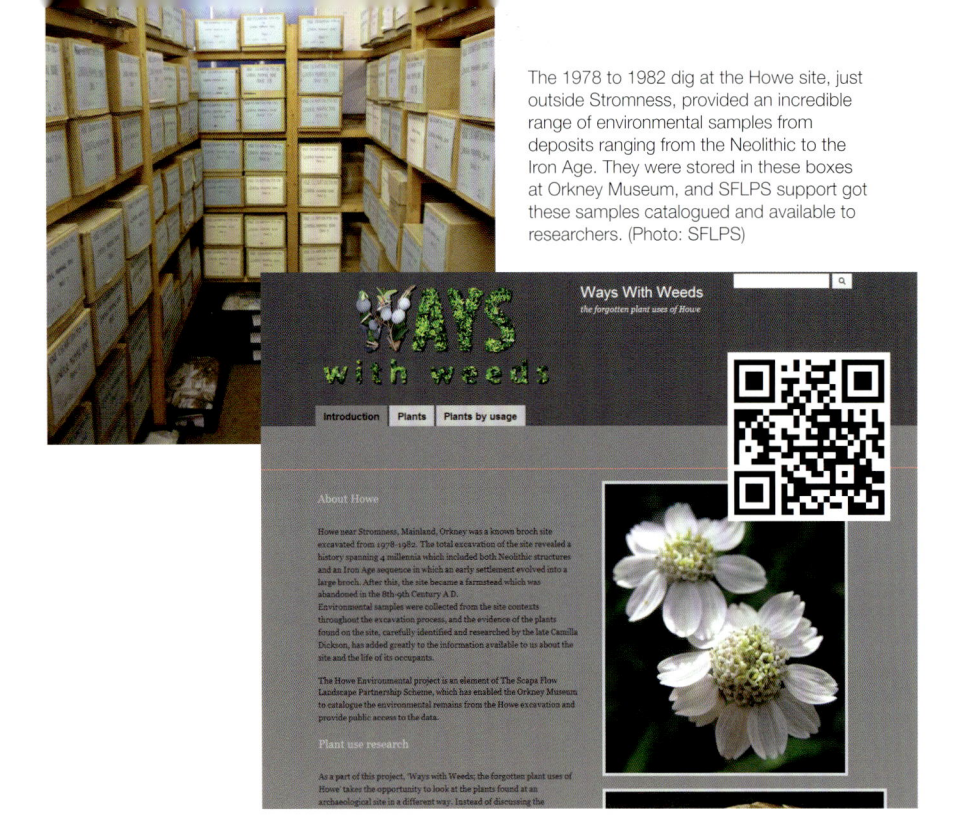

The 1978 to 1982 dig at the Howe site, just outside Stromness, provided an incredible range of environmental samples from deposits ranging from the Neolithic to the Iron Age. They were stored in these boxes at Orkney Museum, and SFLPS support got these samples catalogued and available to researchers. (Photo: SFLPS)

This historic Snelsetter gatepier on South Walls, formerly an important navigation aid, was in a poor state of repair, as this photo shows. The traditional building skills project enabled the gatepier to be restored. (Photo: SFLPS)

Mark Keighley demonstrating the replica Mesolithic fishing spear he created, for permanent display at Tomb of the Eagles. SFLPS supported this exhibition on hunter-gatherer Orkney, created as an extension of the work of Aberdeen University archaeologist Caroline Wickham-Jones and the Rising Tide Project. (Photo: SFLPS)

Not only were the Howe environmental samples catalogued, the Ways With Weeds website was created to provide an online resource detailing the possible uses of the many species of plants known from the Howe samples. (Photo: SFLPS)

The community on Graemsay were keen to know more about the archaeology of their intriguing island, so SFLPS organised for archaeologists from the Orkney Research Centre for Archaeology to spend a day on the island so they could explore its history together. (Photo: Sian Thomas)

The new Story of Flotta displays, putting together photographs and stories from the island's history, are being admired here at the September 2012 SFLPS Stakeholder Forum on the island. (Photo: SFLPS)

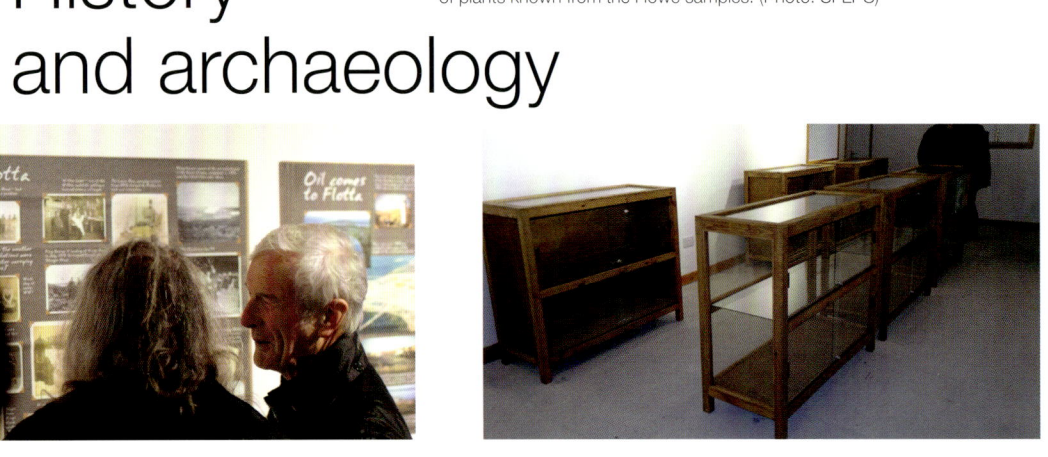

The Story of Flotta exhibition is now on display at the new Lurdy Heritage Centre on Flotta. The Flotta Heritage Trust restored the barn on the end of the Lurdy house, and turned it into a bespoke display space. The many fascinating artefacts on the island needed to be displayed, so local carpenter, Granville Swannay was commissioned to create these beautiful display cases. (Photo: SFLPS)

SFLPS support has enabled repair and repainting of antique farm machinery, along with renewal of the interpretation at the Rendall family's Museums in Rackwick, Hoy. (Photo: SFLPS)

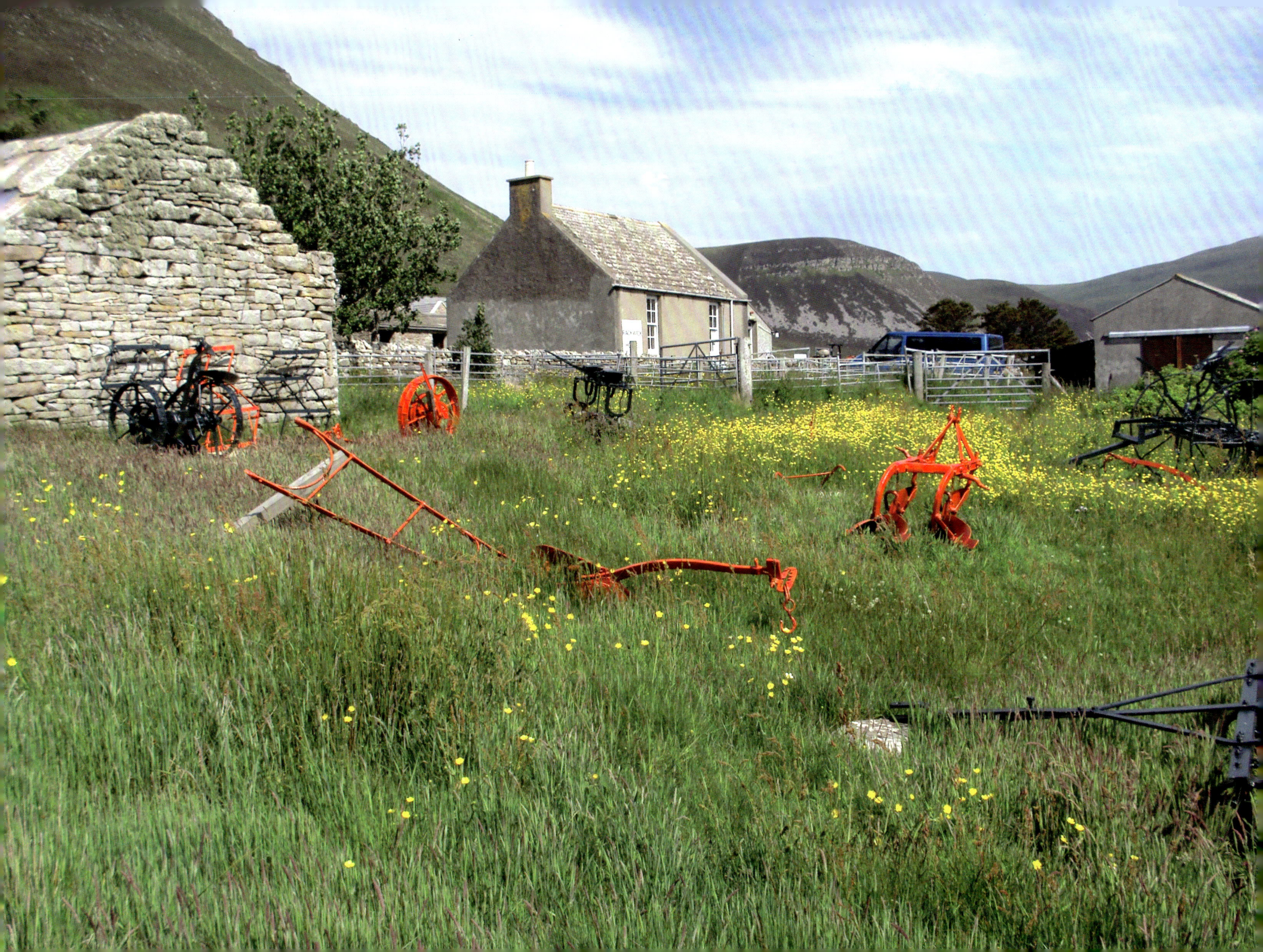

Flotta mural, economics, knitting, digging and dialect

Orkney dialect expert, Tom Rendall, conducted a Scapa Flow Dialect project through structured interviews with people from all around the Flow, such as this interview with Karen Wood in Holm. (Photo: SFLPS)

Training in a range of craft skills extended from formal courses to the provision of materials to enable children at a range of primary schools to be taught to knit by members of the community, as shown here at St Margaret's Hope Primary School. (Photo: SFLPS)

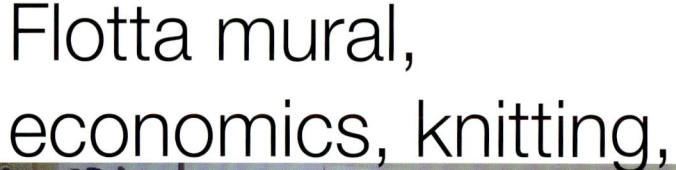

The Economic Life of Scapa Flow exhibition included portraits of the economic contribution made by individuals from around Scapa Flow, as well as panels explaining the function of the Flotta Oil Terminal and outlining the diversity of the local economy. (Artwork: Flagstone Creative)

Not only was Tom's dialect research written up and published, it was also fed back to the communities through a presentation and discussion session, such as this one on Flotta. (Photo: SFLPS)

The Community Archaeology Training course, run by Orkney Research Centre for Archaeology, delivered a very successful training programme in archaeological skills. This included field excavation, as here at Cantick Head. Other fieldwork around Hoy included standing building surveys and investigation of the landscape at Braebuster at the north end of the island, whilst a training dig was also undertaken at The Cairns, Windwick, South Ronaldsay. (Photo: ORCA)

In addition to fieldwork, the Community Archaeology programme included a course on post-excavation analysis at the Archaeology Dept at Orkney College UHI which was also extended to a visit to Orkney Museum to see how archaeological cataloguing works. (Photo: SFLPS)

There was a great deal of very justified pride in Flotta at the results of the community mural project, which was led by Anne Bignall. (Photo: SFLPS)

Whilst looking for the right location for an Economic Life of Scapa Flow exhibition, the SFLPS team was shown the former Flotta school's classroom. Whilst in the end the exhibition went on to be housed at the Waiting Room by the pier on Flotta, it turned out that a community mural highlighting the history of Flotta – the economic history of Scapa Flow in microcosm – was the perfect opportunity to transform the classroom into a community room. (Photo: SFLPS)

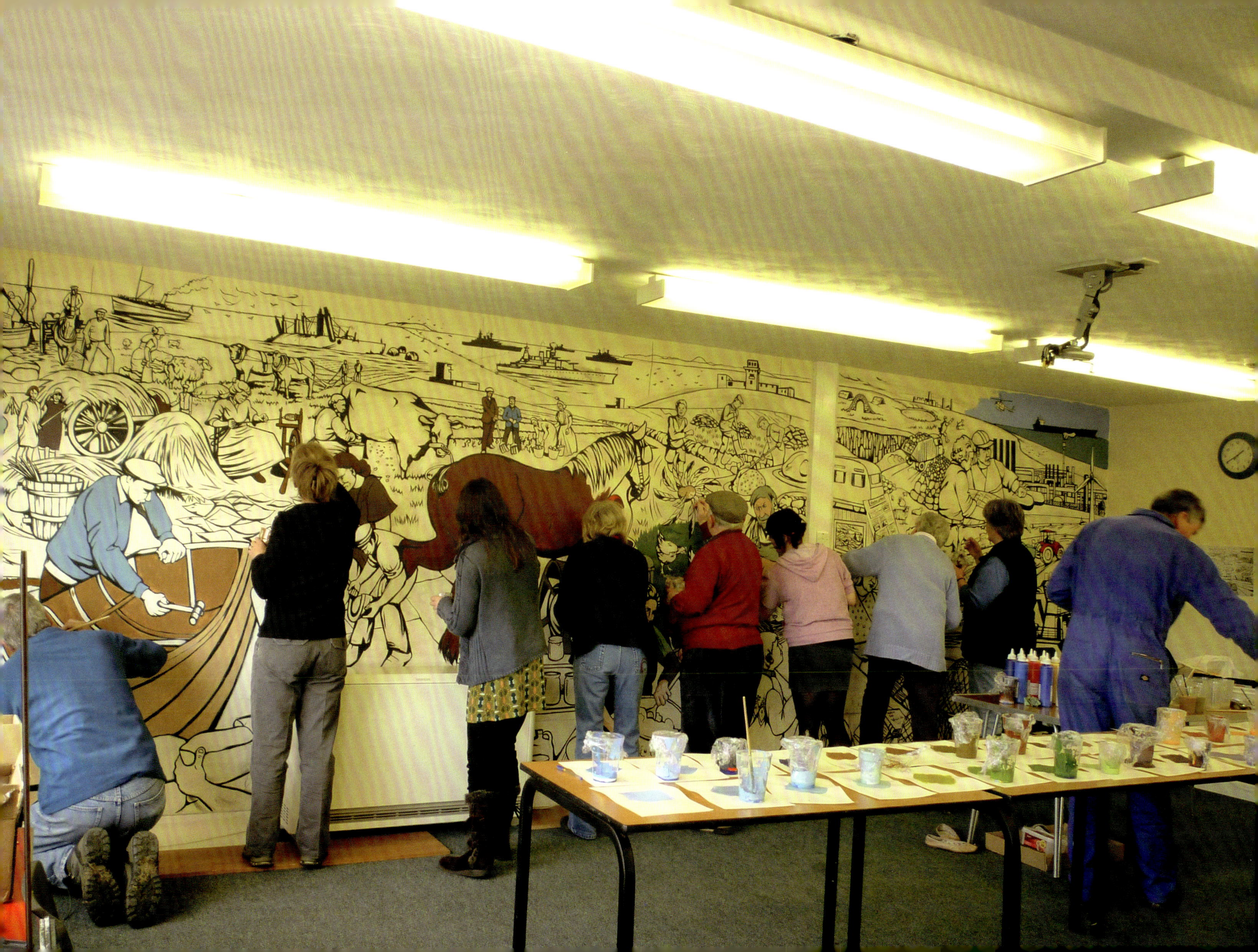

John Rae's fiddle, Flatties, a Cava trip and stonework

This Stromness Primary School trip to uninhabited Cava proved a logistical triumph, letting the local children see first hand the story of depopulation of islands such as Cava, as well as finding this skull from a Sperm Whale which had washed up on the island's shores. (Photo: SFLPS)

Pupils building a Stromness Flattie – the distinctive local dinghy – at Stromness Academy. Under the expert tutelage of boatbuilder Ian Richardson, twelve pupils had the wonderful opportunity to make a Flattie over each of three school years. This was the first one being built in winter 2009/10. (Photo: SFLPS)

The Cava trip also enabled the Stromness Primary School pupils to experience natural habitats and see remains of the WWII defence network. (Photo: SFLPS)

Demand for Frances Pelly's courses on letter-cutting in stone was overwhelming, with repeat courses being run, enabling over 30 participants to have this experience of stone carving. (Photo: SFLPS)

The launch of the second Stromness Flattie. The first two were both launched and given to Orkney Yole Association; the third was put on permanent display at Stromness Academy. (Photo: SFLPS)

Brian Omand ran very successful drystane dyking courses in various locations around Scapa Flow, such as this project on Graemsay. (Photo: SFLPS)

Mark Shiner in his workshop with John Rae's fiddle. Two of Stromness Museum's priceless artefacts were historic fiddles – one a tin fiddle, which saw service in Orkney's herring fishing fleet, and this one which belonged to Arctic explorer John Rae. Both were restored by Mark Shiner through SFLPS support. (Photo: Rebecca Marr)

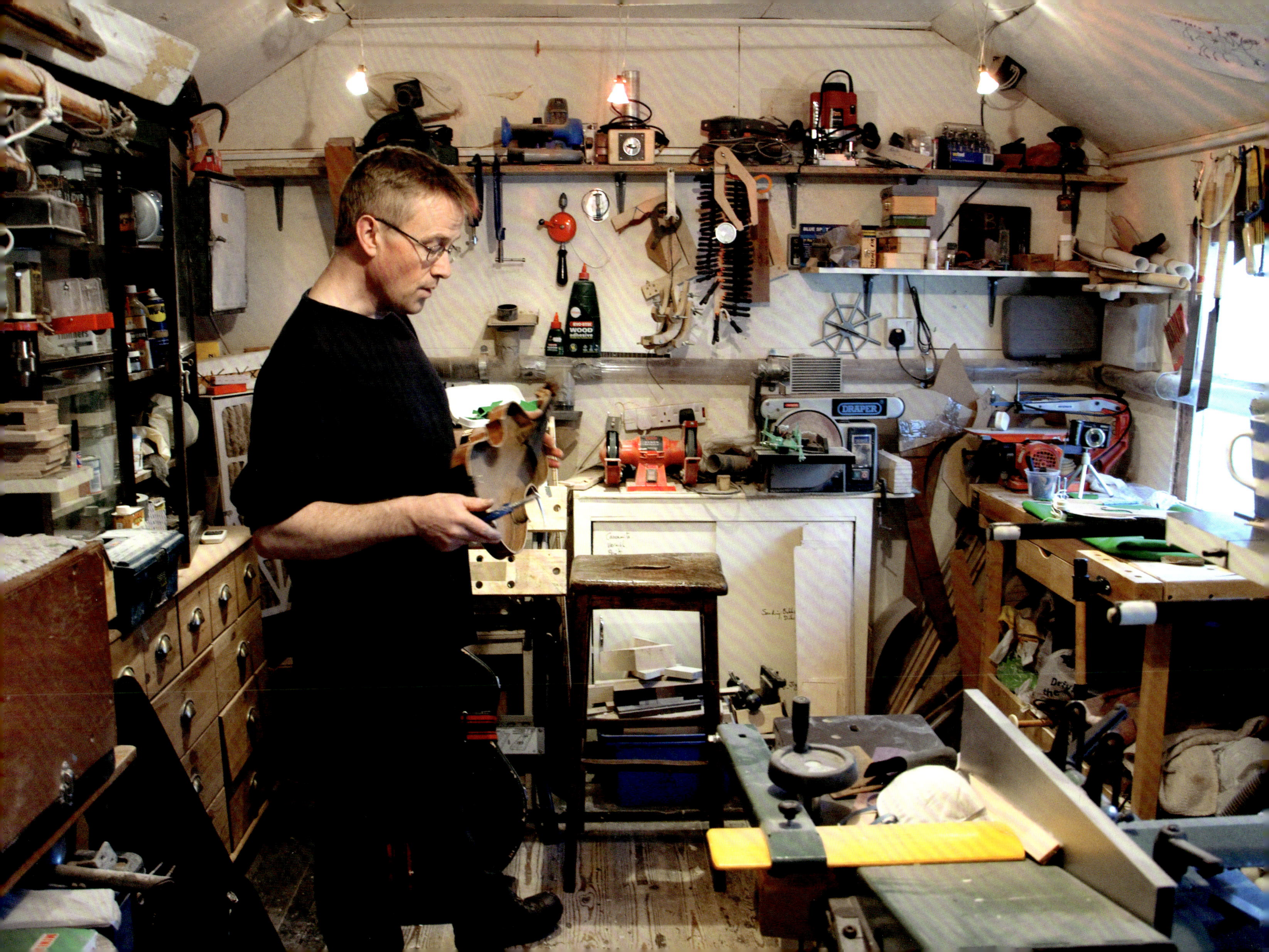
WOOD
adhesive
DRAPER

Creel-making, craft, heritage and lights

The Hoy Kirk was host to a moving evening of warmth and laughter at the premiere of the Hoy Heritage Film, produced by Mark Jenkins through SFLPS support for the Friends of Hoy Kirk. (Photo: Rebecca Marr)

Jewellery-making with isles pupils from the Kirkwall Grammar School hostel was so popular that a second course had to be run. (Photo: Kerry Spence)

The South Ronaldsay Boys' Ploughing Match Committee were concerned about availability of miniature ploughs to keep the match going into the future. Through SFLPS they organised a programme of workshops in 2010 to show people how to make ploughs – this was so successful that there was sufficient demand to repeat the workshop programme 18 months later. (Photo: Moira Budge)

Interpretation about Scapa Flow's lighthouses was put in place on Graemsay, which has the leading lights of Hoy High and Hoy Low, and also in South Walls, where Cantick Head lighthouse stands. (Artwork: Iain Ashman)

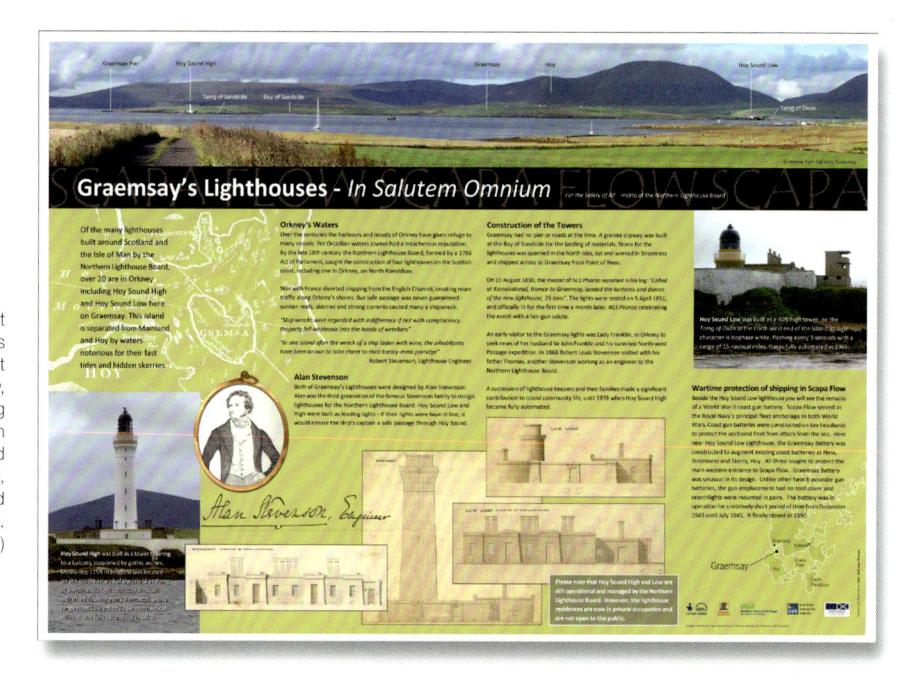

The miniature plough-making was not just for the boys eligible for the ploughing match, with Amy-Jane Budge taking the opportunity to make one herself. (Photo: Moira Budge)

Stromness Museum had a new lighthouses display as a result of SFLPS support, as well as temporary exhibitions, historic violin restoration and new interactive interpretation about marine wildlife. This museum – with its important maritime and natural history collections – draws together an eclectic collection of artefacts and stories. This wonderfully represents the breadth and depth of Scapa Flow's heritage (Photo: SFLPS)

A traditional joinery course produced furniture such as this beautiful chair frame, ready to be made into a straw-backed chair through a follow-on straw-work course. (Photo: Roger Davies)

Peter Leith ran a workshop to make simmans (thatching ropes made from black oat straw) at Corrigall Farm Museum as part of the traditional building skills course. (Photo: SFLPS)

Maritime skills have been essential to Scapa Flow over the years. Here Stewart Shearer shows isles pupils staying at the Kirkwall Grammar School hostel how to make a creel – these have already proved their effectiveness, with one having caught a lobster within weeks. (Photo: Robert MacNamara)

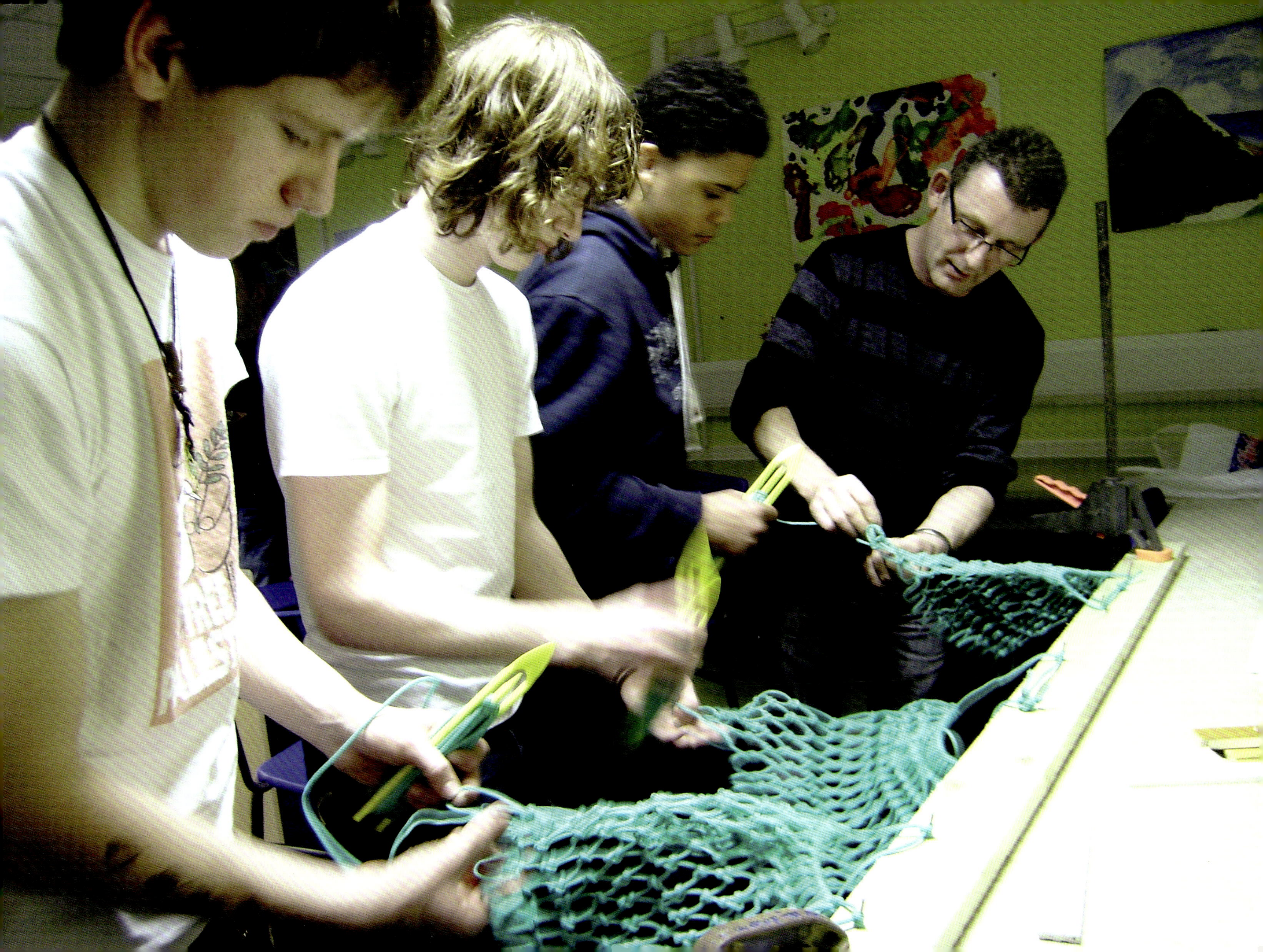

James Sinclair and the Hoy Kirk

The Hoy Kirk was the venue for the James Sinclair exhibition, as well as a host of other activities supported through SFLPS. The Friends of Hoy Kirk are taking the Kirk from strength to strength as a heritage centre and community venue. (Photo: SFLPS)

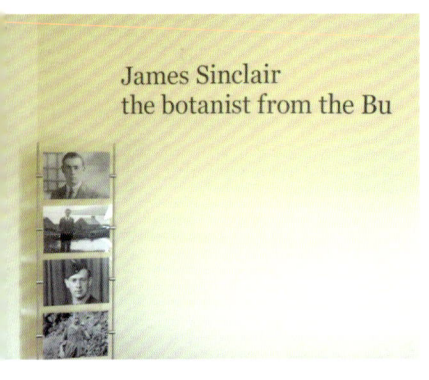

James Sinclair was a Hoy botanist who became better known for his work in the Far East as Curator of the Singapore Botanical Garden's Herbarium in the mid 20th Century. (Photo: Rebecca Marr)

The walk in the footsteps of James Sinclair was blessed with wonderful weather, with interesting plants from the outset, such as this colony of Field Gentian. (Photo: Rebecca Marr)

Cotton-grass was in full bloom, and a new site for Small White Orchid was discovered. (Photo: Rebecca Marr)

The satisfaction on John Crossley's face is apparent as he takes members of James' family, other local people and a range of Orkney naturalists to the natural history treasures of Skecking Gill. (Photo: Rebecca Marr)

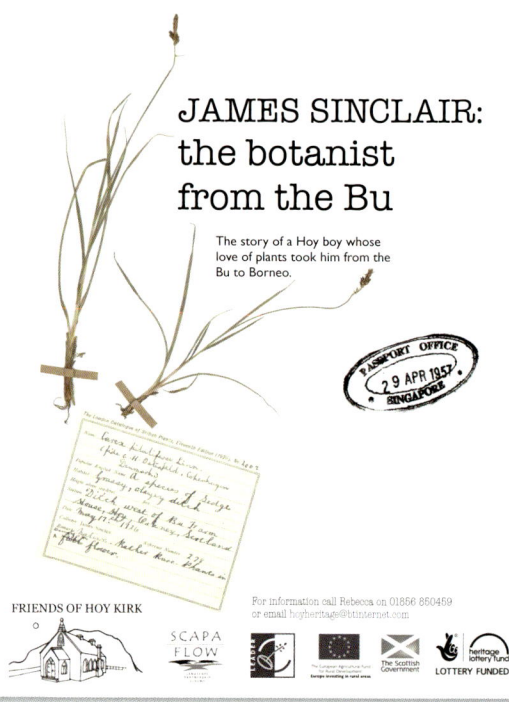

Hoy Kirk was a great venue for a very diverse range of activity through the Arts & Crafts Workshop project. (Photo: Rebecca Marr)

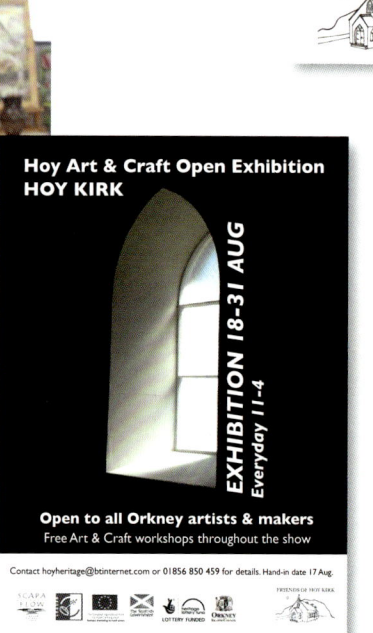

Exhibition at Hoy Kirk
Open all Summer

JAMES SINCLAIR: the botanist from the Bu

The story of a Hoy boy whose love of plants took him from the Bu to Borneo.

The launch of the James Sinclair exhibition ensured that his contributions to botany were remembered in Hoy, and also threw a spotlight on the wonderful flora of Hoy which inspired James as a young man. Despite being a minor project in terms of budget and activity, it had considerable impact. (Artwork: Rebecca Marr)

The Arts & Crafts Workshops project culminated in a well-supported Open Exhibition. (Artwork: Rebecca Marr).

James Sinclair's life and work was celebrated by a walk in his footsteps, up Skecking Gill on the flanks of Cuilags on Hoy, to see rare and beautiful Arctic-Alpine plants. Here walk leader John Crossley leads the way to the realm of the Purple Saxifrage and Moss Campion. (Photo: Rebecca Marr)

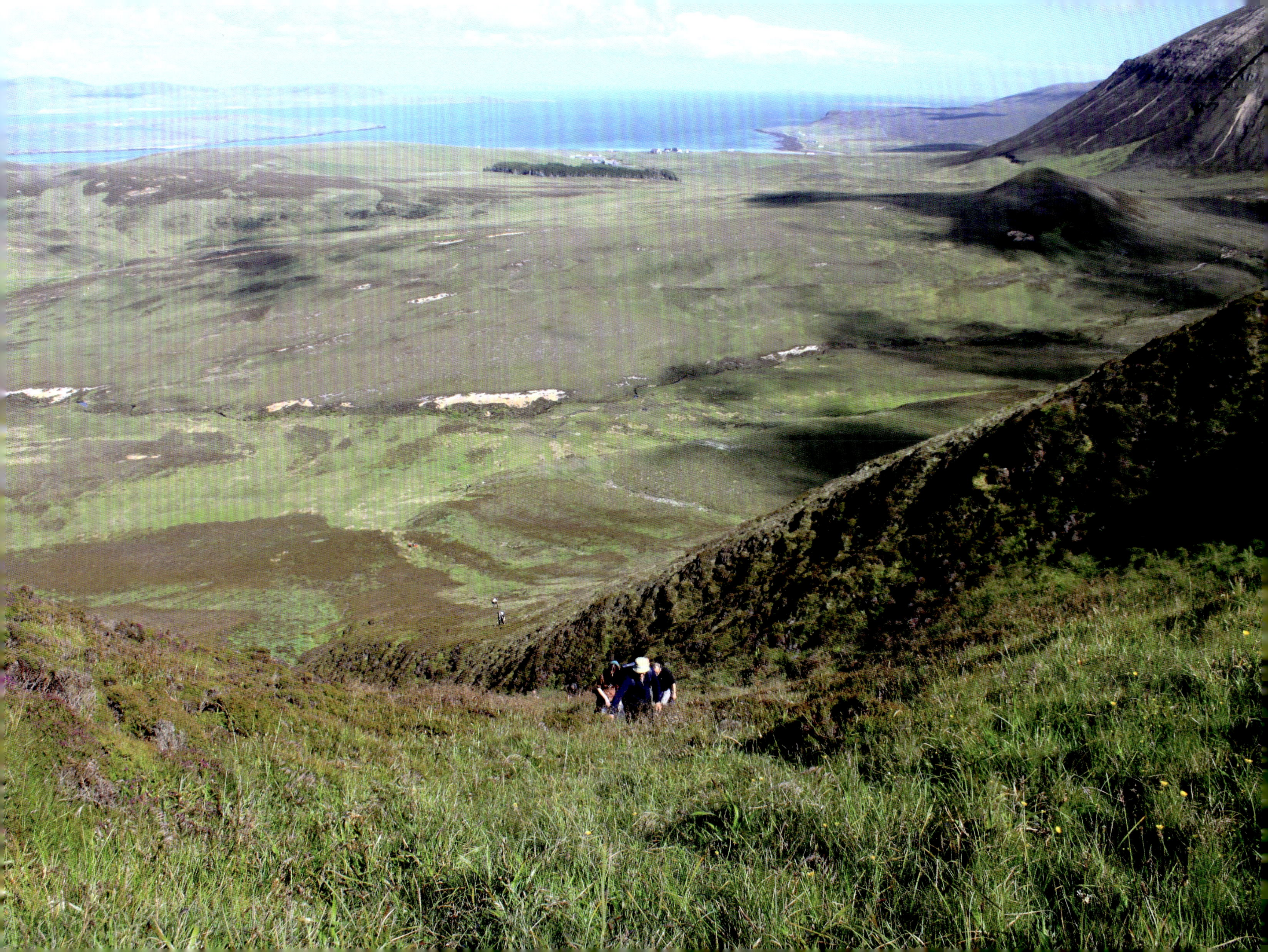

BAG THAT BRUCK, BEUY!

Bag the Bruck is a community initiative run by Environmental Concern Orkney, which involves hundreds in beach cleans all around Orkney each spring. SFLPS worked with ECO to promote Bag the Bruck, and this cartoon was commissioned for canvas bags which were given out to those taking part. (Artwork: Alex Leonard)

Sue Whitworth of the RSPB worked with several of Orkney's primary schools to develop a marine litter education pack and raise awareness of how plastic can kill sealife. This culminated in a play called All Washed Up performed by local children at the Orkney International Science Festival in September 2009. (Photo: Sue Whitworth)

This bench, made from a pile of rough granite blocks strewn on Brinkie's Brae, was designed by Frances Pelly and built by George Louttit. Frances carved a haiku by Yvonne Gray into a flagstone which is now set into the ground in front of the bench – "A lark spills song / to the restless earth. / Among old stones / fresh shoots stir". A wonderful vista of Scapa Flow treats the eye of anyone who sits here, having climbed up the steep heathery slope from Stromness. (Photo: Frances Pelly)

Orkney has some amazing wildlife... ...marine litter takes its toll every day... ...and spoils our beautiful islands

'A guillemot, found dead on Scapa beach, had 152 pieces of plastic in its intestinal tract, gut and stomach - causing it a slow and agonising death!'

'Orkney volunteers on shore collect 15% of marine litter, but another 15% floats on the surface of the sea and a massive 70% sinks under the water causing havoc to marine wildlife.'

'This is a man-made problem. Every piece of litter has an owner and we all need to take responsibility to not drop litter in the first place.'

Please help our fantastic bruckbusting volunteers and join our efforts to....

Bag the Bruck
Sat 16th & Sun 17th April 2011
for more details visit:
www.eco-orkney.org.uk
or phone: 01856 761230

cleaner safer better

This is one of the adverts put in The Orcadian to advertise Bag the Bruck. An on-line leaflet was also produced to highlight the terrible global problem of marine litter whilst showing how local action can make a difference. (Artwork: Iain Ashman)

The Old Man of Hoy footpath was greatly improved by an RSPB project to provide drainage and resurfacing using material from the line of the path. The walk to Orkney's most iconic landmark is now much easier, and this has been achieved with the minimum of impact to the sensitive moorland habitat it runs through. (Photo: RSPB)

Bugs, bruck and paths

Interpretation panels and walks leaflets were produced to promote Scapa Flow's coastal walks and to identify the heritage highlights of each. This panel at the end of the Ayre as you go onto South Walls tells of the fantastic scenery and wildlife to be encountered if you walk along the south coast from there to Cantick Head. (Photo: SFLPS).

Dramatic coastal scenery is also to be encountered along the west coast of South Ronaldsay, between Burwick and Sandwick. SFLPS improved the access along this section of coast, with this marker post at Sandwick pointing the way to what must be one of Orkney's best walks. (Photo: SFLPS)

Rebecca Marr, Hoy Kirk Heritage Officer, and Elaine Batchelor, South Isles Ranger, identified that the visitor maps by the piers at Moaness and Lyness in Hoy, needed updating. SFLPS could cover the costs of this, and Rebecca and Elaine worked with designer Iain Ashman to create stunning and informative visitor panels. (Artwork: Iain Ashman)

The SFLPS funding brought natural history experts to Orkney so they could share their skills and assist with biological recording. Here national bug expert Pete Kirby goes through his catch on Hoy in July 2011. (Photo: Sarah Lambert)

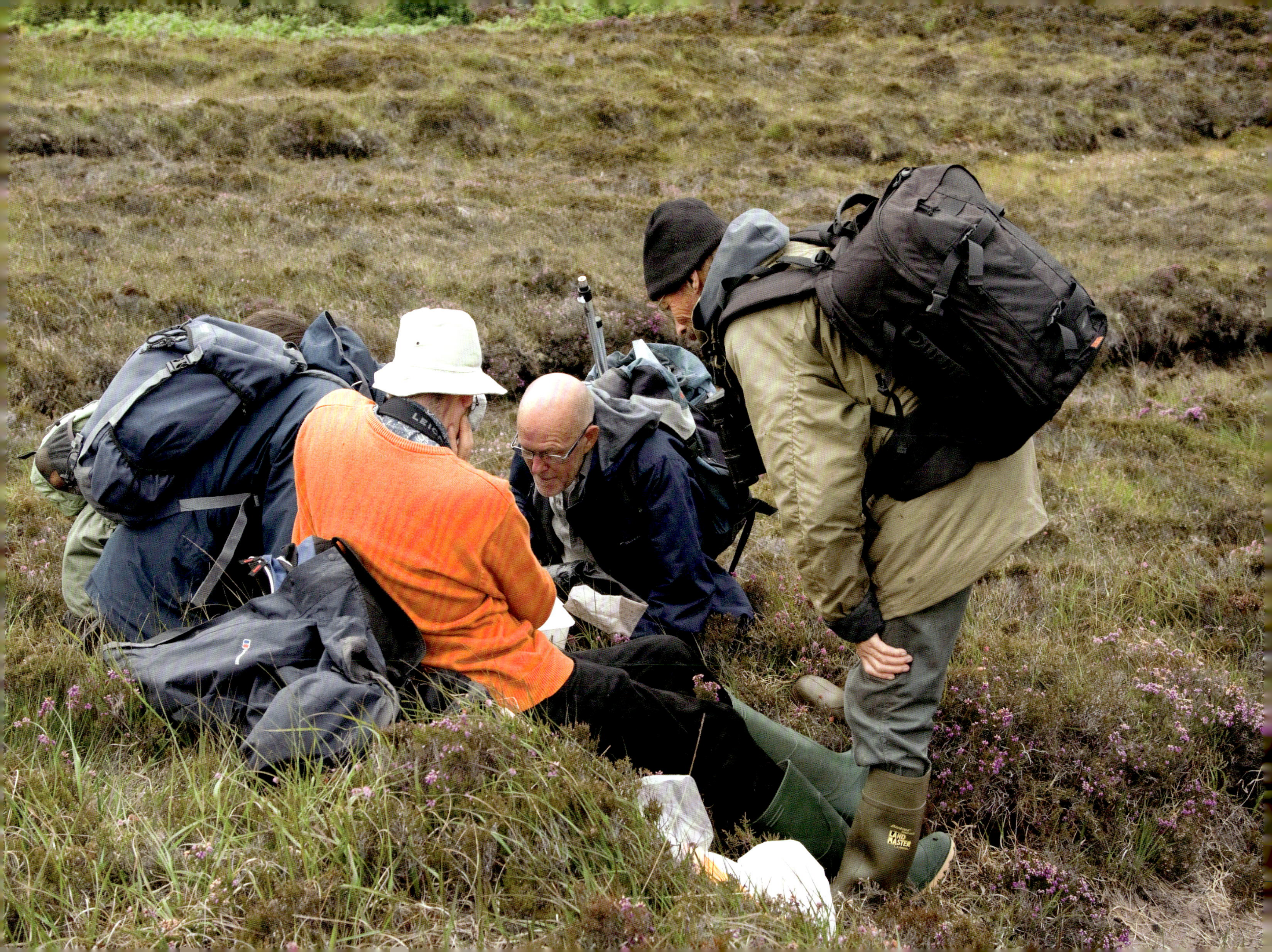
LAND MASTER

Orkney Skate Trust conservation fishing trip for Flapper Skate. This huge fish was once ubiquitous around the north-east Atlantic coast, but Orkney is now one of its two remaining strongholds. It is considered Critically Endangered, a status which recognises this species as being in even greater danger of extinction than the Blue Whale or Giant Panda. (Photo: Orkney Skate Trust)

Work in progress to re-roof Bankburn Cottage, which was in serious danger of collapse. The decision to designate Happy Valley as a Local Nature Reserve, and the opportunity to use this building as an exemplar in traditional roofing practice, enabled SFLPS to invest heavily in this important work. (Photo: SFLPS)

SFLPS could cover the costs of wildlife surveys and habitat management work at Happy Valley, but the other priority was repairing and improving the paths around this enchanting site. These new steps and burnside pathwork have just been reinstated by Magnus Johnstone. (Photo: SFLPS)

More work by Magnus was to repair the revetment wall around this meander of the burn, preventing the path being eroded away. (Photo: SFLPS)

This Flapper Skate has just been caught unharmed, and was on-board for as long as it took to mark it with a uniquely-numbered plastic tag, as part of the mark-release-recapture study into this rare species, organised by Orkney Skate Trust. (Photo: Orkney Skate Trust)

Happy Valley, skate and trees

The conifer plantation around the World War II naval cinema on Flotta was the focus of a programme of woodland management funded by SFLPS. Here local people plant new saplings to ensure the future of this plantation, which was originally created by naval ratings during WWII. (Photo: SFLPS)

The interpretation panel at the Flotta plantation, on a plinth built by Ronnie Spence, was the first to be created under the Scheme. (Photo: SFLPS)

Brian Ribbands carefully collects samples from a population of Aspen, a native tree which hangs on – quite literally in this case – around Scapa Flow's coastline and cliffs. These samples were then cloned and grown on, to provide indigenous stock for planting out in new native woodlands around Orkney. (Photo: Jenny Taylor)

Bankburn Cottage, Happy Valley, on a frosty day just after the building was repaired and re-roofed in a traditional style. For fifty years this was the home of Edwin Harrold, creator of the woodland garden of Happy Valley. (Photo: SFLPS)

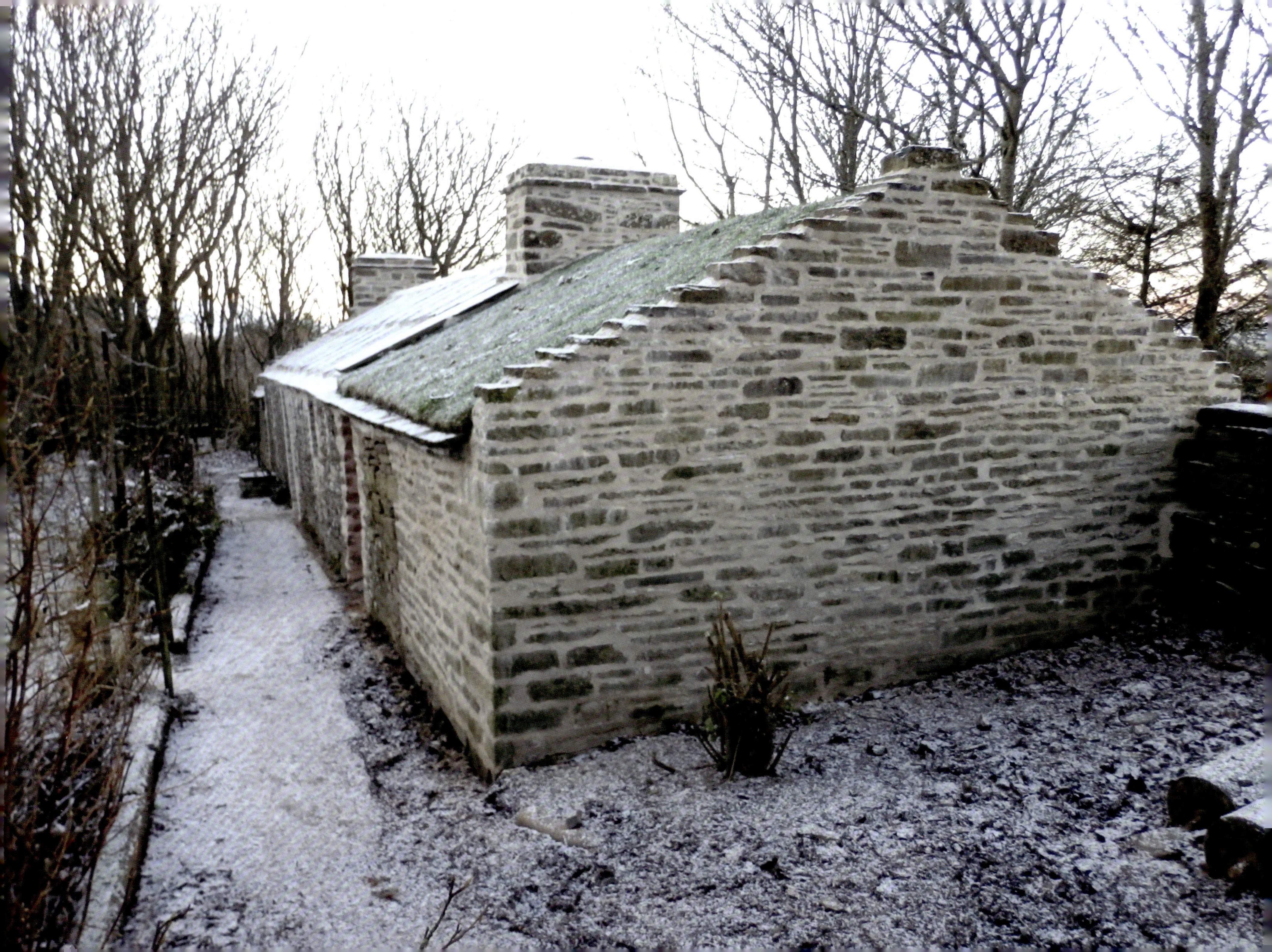

Marine week and community film

The finale of the SFLPS Marine Week in June 2012 was a charter of the mv *Pentalina*, to take over 200 lucky people around Scapa Flow in an unique cruise. (Photo: Sydney Gauld)

The packed decks of the *Pentalina* gave excellent views of the stunning coastline, with wildlife highlights of the trip including Manx Shearwaters and Black-throated Divers. (Photo: SFLPS)

Tim Dean and Tom Muir provided the commentary on the *Pentalina* cruise, as they did on many charter trips using Orkney Ferries' mv *Graemsay* to take school parties or the public around Scapa Flow. Tim and Tom provided an excellent combination of local knowledge and wildlife and cultural expertise, ensuring that every trip they ran was both informative and entertaining. (Photo: SFLPS)

Sunday 10th June
Tour Scapa Flow
on the
MV Pentalina

A 3-hour afternoon tour (2pm - 5pm) of Scapa Flow, exploring the history and wildlife of the 'Great Harbour'

Starting at St Margaret's Hope, our route will circumnavigate 'the Flow' passing key wartime sites including coast batteries, the Churchill Barriers Lyness Naval Headquarters and the HMS Vanguard and HMS Royal Oak buoys. En route we'll be experiencing dramatic coastal scenery and looking out for birdlife, seals, whales, dolphins and porpoises.

Cost: Adults £20   Under 16s £10   Under 5s Free
Booking essential.
Call Pentland Ferries on 0800 688 8998

The Marine Week included the opportunity to try snorkelling, with Anne Bignall, Penny Martin and Scapa Scuba making sure that adults and children could have an introduction to the world of underwater wildlife. The packed programme for the week also included conservation angling trips, varied talks covering subjects from eelgrass to seaweed, seals and skate, and low tide walks to look at inter-tidal sealife. (Photo: SFLPS)

A priority of SFLPS was to ensure that the project work genuinely engaged the local community. Careful planning of the scheme's work, with early consultation meetings, one-to-one consultation and project development undertaken by James Green in 2008, and ongoing involvement and consultation throughout the 2009 to 2012 implementation phase of the scheme, was central to this. In addition there was an annual Stakeholder Forum which brought all parties together. This photo shows the afternoon excursion of the 2011 Stakeholder Forum, which went around Hoxa Head with the kind permission of landowner John Thomson. (Photo: SFLPS)

Glaitness Primary School has developed the Pick Up 3 Pieces campaign to tackle beach litter around the year. The School made this art display for the Marine Week from the profusion of beach litter on Scapa Beach, to raise awareness of this serious issue. (Photo: SFLPS)

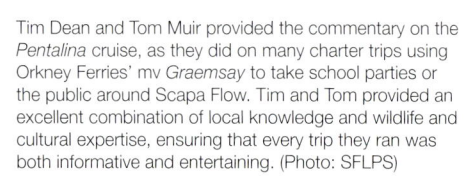

The Pier Arts Centre worked with SFLPS to commission a community arts project. Mark Jenkins' proposal to create a film *The Imaginary Worlds of Scapa Flow* won the commission, and the premiere at Cromarty Hall, St Margaret's Hope, was a sell out. (Photo: Rebecca Marr)

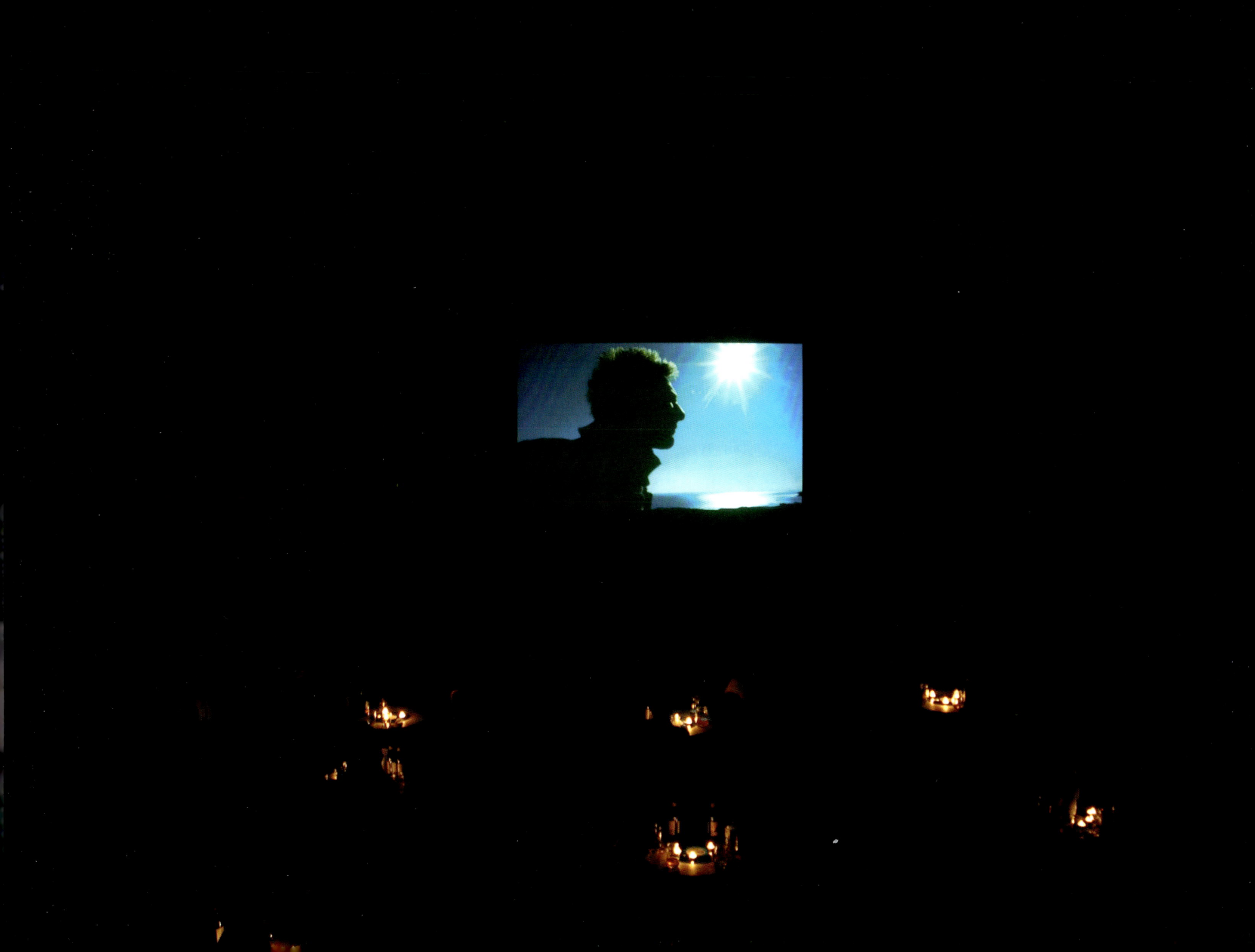

Boat trips, teaching and Scapa Flow online

The mv *Graemsay* proved a great boat to take school parties around Scapa Flow. Ingredients to the success included the patience of the crew, excellent commentary on the wildlife and history and copies of the 1943 map of Scapa Flow's defences, which brought alive the network of defence infrastructure that kept the Home Fleet safe in their World War II anchorage. (Photo: SFLPS)

SFLPS set out to produce a website which documented the range of heritage around Scapa Flow. The scale of this task proved enormous, but in the end, the work of Joyce Gray, other SFLPS staff and a whole host of contributors enabled www.scapaflow.co to be launched.

Trips to the Pentland Skerries provided superb close views of the puffins. (Photo: SFLPS)

The mv *Sheila C*, run by Magnus Spence and Magnus Woolham, was the perfect boat for small boat trips to Switha, Fara and Cava. The trips were enlivened further by seeing what Magnus Spence brought to the surface from his dives in search of scallops. (Photo: SFLPS)

An excellent Education Pack, focussing on Wartime Orkney, was produced by Sheila Faichney through SFLPS. Fran Flett Hollinrake then delivered a course to train teachers in the use of the pack, starting with making carrot muffins to a WWII recipe in Kirkwall, followed by a field trip to Ness Battery. (Photo: SFLPS)

The mv *Graemsay* cruises past Cava and Fara on an SFLPS charter on a moody day in Scapa Flow. (SFLPS)